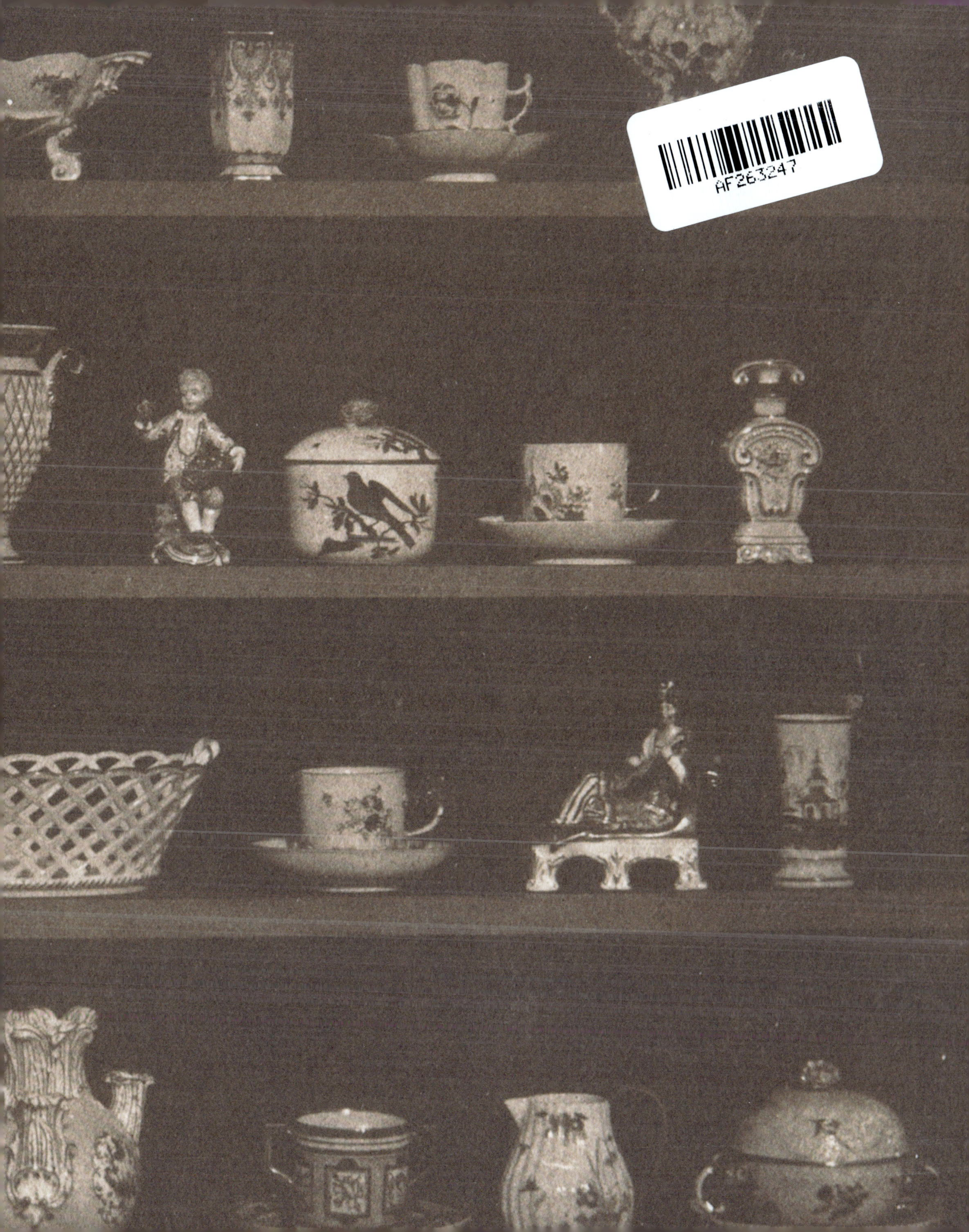
AF263247

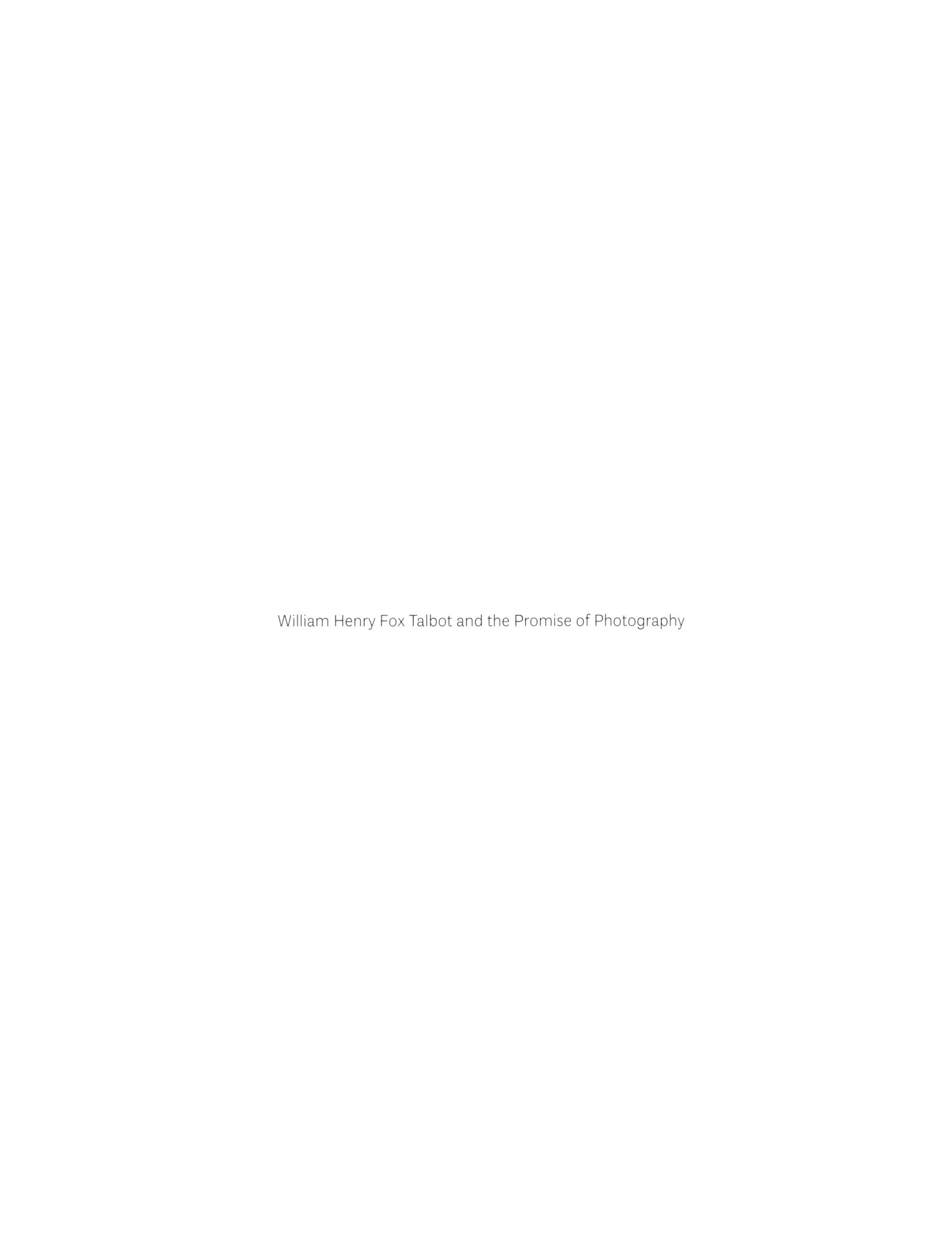

William Henry Fox Talbot and the Promise of Photography

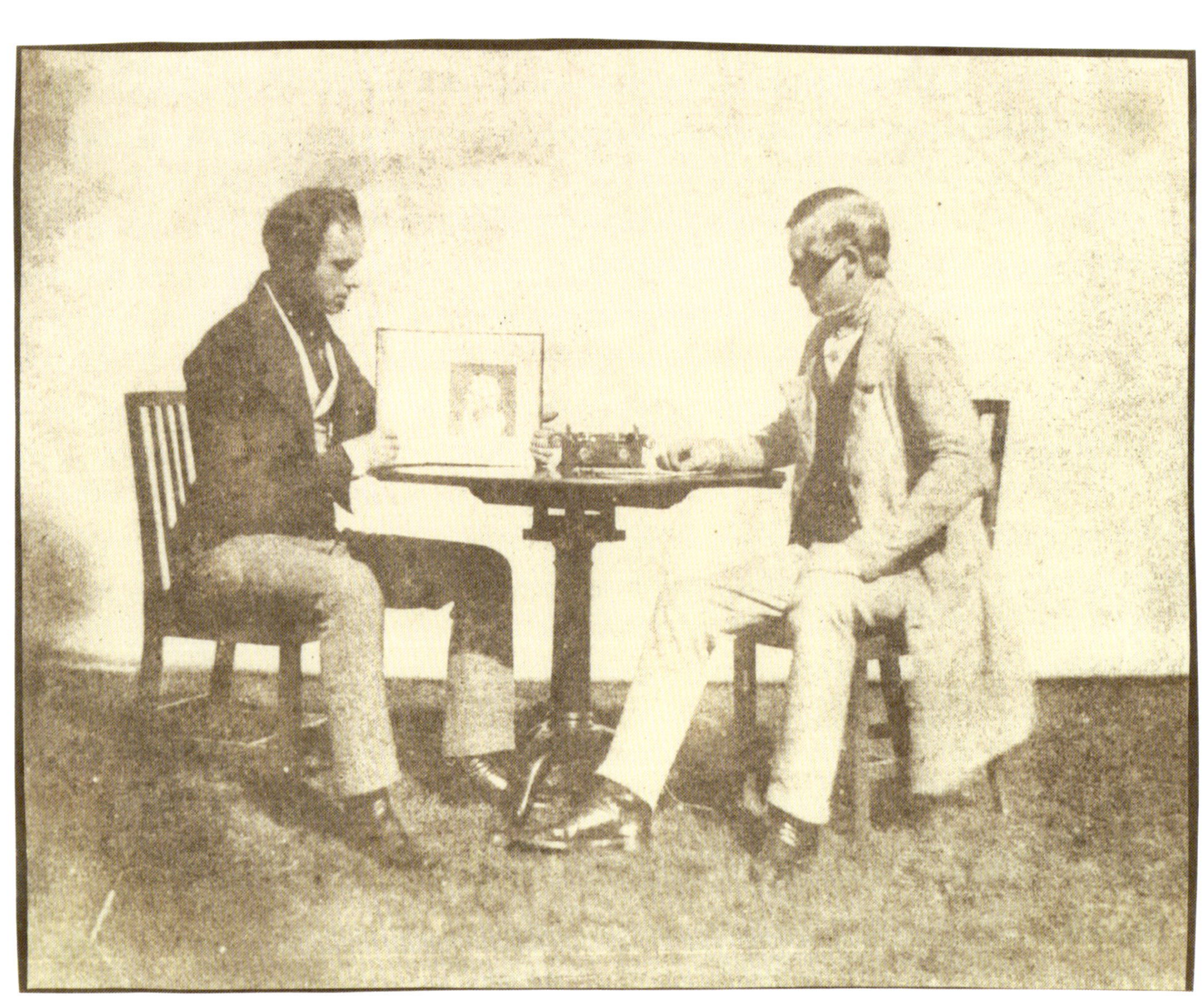

WILLIAM HENRY FOX TALBOT AND THE PROMISE OF PHOTOGRAPHY

DAN LEERS with contributions by LARRY J. SCHAAF

CARNEGIE MUSEUM of ART

Pittsburgh, Pennsylvania

DIRECTOR'S FOREWORD

The British polymath William Henry Fox Talbot invented photography's negative/positive process in 1839, and with it, the possibility of generating multiple images from a single negative. With his innovation, he established the foundation for the medium as it existed for most of the nineteenth and twentieth centuries. It is our great pleasure at Carnegie Museum of Art to present his work for the first time in Pittsburgh.

This publication and the exhibition it accompanies were inspired and supported by the generosity of William Talbott Hillman, a close friend of the museum, a photographer himself, and a highly knowledgeable collector. Bill's keen eye and deep understanding of what makes a good picture are felt in his collection, which he began to amass in the 1980s and which includes many of the most recognizable pictures in the history of photography. He has expressed a desire to share his collection, and the photographs in this exhibition and book are evidence of that. Furthermore, Bill's donation of seven works by Talbot or members of his circle, combined with a promised gift of four additional photographs and his Foundation's support for the purchase of four more, mean that Carnegie Museum of Art now has the largest Talbot collection in Pennsylvania. We couldn't be more grateful.

Having amassed such strong holdings, it was natural for us to want to organize a show and book in celebration of Talbot's remarkable achievement. Talbot was ahead of his time; he knew that the applications for a medium that could instantly and accurately record a scene, a person, or an event were limitless. He combined his extensive knowledge of art, botany, chemistry, optics, and a host of other subjects to invent photography on paper that was endlessly reproducible and easily shareable. This innovation eclipsed a rival process of the time—the more laborious daguerreotype, which was printed on a metal sheet. Talbot's desire to link photography with many other art forms parallels a cross-disciplinary spirit that drives many museums today.

Dan Leers, our curator of photography, worked closely with Bill Hillman and his team to bring this project to fruition. Dan's tireless work in researching the period and securing key loans and his contributions to the catalogue greatly illuminate the photographer's varied interests. Lenders to the exhibition were crucial to this endeavor, and we are very grateful to those who kindly agreed to part with important works for the duration of the exhibition.

William Henry Fox Talbot and the Promise of Photography marks an important occasion for Carnegie Museum of Art and for Pittsburgh. As the newest curatorial department at the museum, photography is asserting its presence. It is fitting that we feature work that dates to the dawn of the medium, yet still feels relevant. Talbot was obsessed with the notion of fixing an image on paper; for him permanence was critical. Today, anyone with a smartphone can take a picture. Yet those digital images are so quickly swiped off our screens and dispersed into the cloud that we barely have time to register them. In contrast, Talbot's pictures remain with us both literally and figuratively. They take us back to another time, making his milieu, its light and weather, almost palpable. This exhibition honors Talbot's remarkable invention and his prescient understanding of the medium's almost unending potential.

Lynn Zelevansky
Henry J. Heinz II Director

WILLIAM HENRY FOX TALBOT
and the **PROMISE** of **PHOTOGRAPHY**

DAN LEERS

*The phaenomenon which I have now briefly mentioned appears
to me to partake of the character of the marvellous, almost as
much as any fact which physical investigation has yet brought to
our knowledge. The most transitory of things, a shadow,
the proverbial emblem of all that is fleeting and momentary,
may be fettered by the spells of our "natural magic,"
and may be fixed for ever in the position which it seemed only
destined for a single instant to occupy.*
—William Henry Fox Talbot[1]

Victorian "gentlemen scientists" working in Britain in the mid-nineteenth
century performed experiments and made discoveries with little concern for
financial gain. For them, knowing that they had advanced a field of study or
invented a device that improved modern life was often reward enough.
William Henry Fox Talbot (British, 1800–1877) was just such a person
[FIG. 1]. His investigations into mathematics, optics, and chemistry, combined with his knowledge of botany, art, foreign languages, and classics, led
to his invention of paper photography. This volume gathers a selection of
Talbot's early photographs, divided into themes that mirror these myriad
interests. Taken together, the pictures allude to Talbot's belief, now vindi-
cated, that photography held the promise to change the world.

1 William Henry Fox Talbot, "Some Account
of the Art of Photogenic Drawing, or
the Process by Which Natural Objects
May Be Made to Delineate Themselves
without the Aid of the Artist's Pencil,"
paper read before the Royal Society,
London, January 31, 1839; published
in *London and Edinburgh Philosophical*
Magazine and Journal of Science 14,
no. 87 (March 1839).

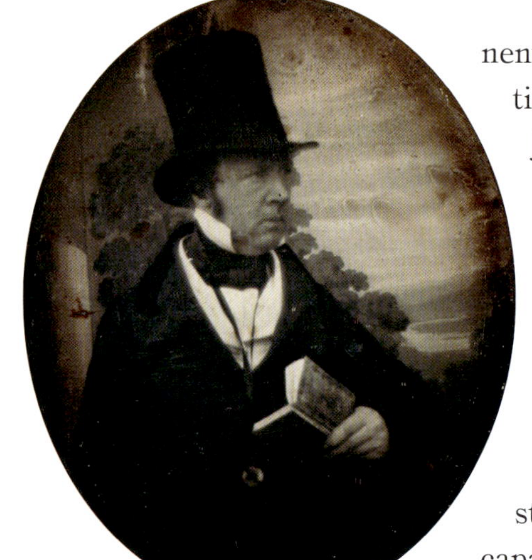

Though not the first to permanently capture an image—that distinction belongs to the Frenchman Louis Jacques Mandé Daguerre—Talbot was the first to do so on a piece of paper. While daguerreotypes fell out of fashion shortly after their release in 1839, Talbot's work formed the basis of photography for most of the nineteenth and twentieth centuries. At an early stage, Talbot understood that the capacity to quickly and economically reproduce an image multiple times would fundamentally change visual arts and publishing. And while his socioeconomic status meant he had the luxury of not worrying about whether this invention was lucrative, Talbot was aware that photography's ability to alter how people perceived their world was priceless.

Born into a well-known family descended from the Earls of Ilchester and with connections to British royalty, Talbot nevertheless did not have an easy early life. His father, William Davenport Talbot, died when Henry was only five months old, leaving the family with massive debt and nowhere to live. His mother, Lady Elisabeth (née Fox-Strangways), was a smart and resourceful woman who did everything she could to insulate the family from hardship. They relied on the generosity of relatives for housing and support for several years until Lady Elisabeth met and married Captain Charles Feilding, a naval officer, in 1804.

Talbot was a precocious child. From the age of eight, he instructed his family to save all his correspondence, perhaps sensing that he was destined for greatness. He began his formal education at Rottingdean in

Sussex, before entering London's Harrow School in 1811 under the tutelage of the headmaster, Dr. George Butler. There, he identified several subjects that would sustain him for the rest of his life: he learned botany and wrote a catalogue of *The Flora and Fauna of Harrow* (1812) and won several prizes for mathematics. Eventually, Talbot's intellectual abilities and appetites surpassed the offerings of Harrow, and when he was fifteen he was encouraged to leave the school.

After a few years of private tutoring, Talbot entered Trinity College, Cambridge, where he studied mathematics and classics. A university classmate, speaking of Talbot's devotion to his studies, recalled, "He is very laborious, not so much I think out of vanity or even ambition as from the mere love of what he is acquiring. He has an innate love of knowledge, and rushes towards it as an otter does to a pond. He bids fair to be a distinguished man."[2] Indeed, Talbot thought it important to have wide-ranging interests both to be a well-rounded scholar and to ward off potential boredom. In a letter to his stepfather, he wrote, "I told you in my last letter, I had been solacing myself with my Astronomy. There is nothing like having two or three different pursuits for *se délasser* [relaxation] when anything goes wrong."[3]

In 1821 Talbot earned his BA from Cambridge and turned twenty-one, meaning he now had full access to his family's estate and the means to do more as he pleased. He pursued a passion for travel, making several trips to the European continent over the coming years. In 1824, while visiting Munich, he met the noted British scholar John Herschel. Their eventual friendship would result in many discussions and experiments that proved pivotal to the development of photography. In 1825 Talbot also spent several weeks interning at the Paris Observatory alongside astronomer François Arago, another individual who would play a role in the invention of photography, this time in France.

At the age of twenty-seven, Talbot received the welcome news that he could now take up permanent residence in his family homestead,

2   John William Ward, *Letters of The Earl of Dudley to The Bishop of Llandaff* (London: John Murray, 1840), 298.

3   Talbot to Charles Feilding, April 8, 1821, British Library, London; transcribed in *The Correspondence of William Henry Fox Talbot*, Doc. No. 922, http://foxtalbot.dmu.ac.uk (hereafter, *Correspondence*).

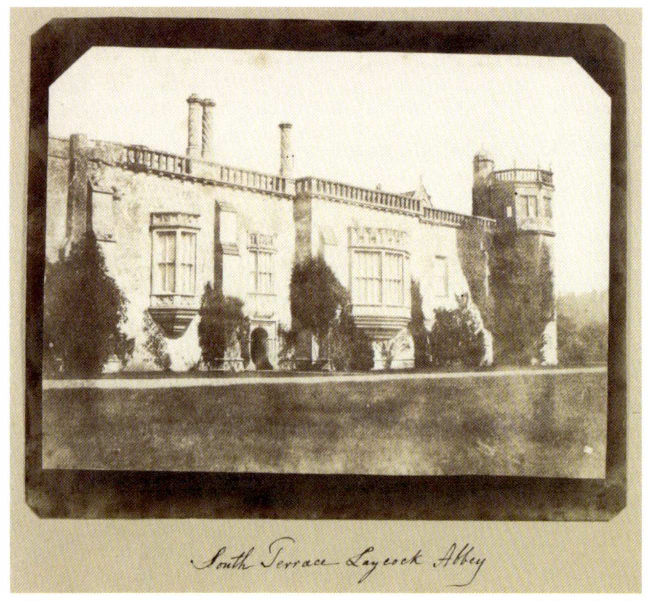

FIG. 2

South Front of Lacock Abbey towards Sharington's Tower, 1842–43
Salted paper print from a calotype negative
6⅛ × 8⁵⁄₁₆ in. (15.5 × 21.1 cm) image; 7³⁄₁₆ × 8⅞ in. (18.3 × 22.5 cm) sheet
National Science & Media Museum, Bradford

Lacock Abbey in Wiltshire. The Abbey would henceforth serve as Talbot's home and laboratory [FIG. 2]. With ample space to think and work, he published his first novel, *Legendary Tales in Verse and Prose*, in 1830 and was nominated as a Fellow of the Royal Society (Britain's preeminent scientific organization) in 1831. He became a Member of Parliament for the region on a reform platform in 1832, though he came to loathe politics. His personal life also would flourish with his marriage to Constance Mundy that same year.

A trip to Europe in 1833 would prove fateful to Talbot's development of photography. At Lake Como in Italy, while Constance, a talented amateur artist, made sketches of the beautiful vistas, Talbot became dissatisfied with his own attempts, despite using an optical device to assist him. This led him, he later recounted, "to reflect on the inimitable beauty of the pictures of nature's painting which the glass lens of the Camera [lucida] throws upon the paper in its focus—fairy pictures, creations of a moment, and destined as rapidly to fade away. It was during these thoughts that the idea occurred to me…how charming it would be if it were possible to cause these natural images to imprint themselves durably and remain fixed upon the paper!"[4]

Talbot returned home in January 1834 excited by the prospect of "imprinting" images. He drew on his own knowledge of chemistry but also relied on others' experiments, notably Johann Heinrich Schulze's discovery in the eighteenth century of the light sensitivity of silver nitrate. Talbot used various silver-based solutions to coat paper and then exposed it to light. By February 1835 he had successfully recorded the outlines of different objects on paper using a process he first called "sciagraphic" (having to do with shadows and shading) and then "photogenic" (having to do with light). Today, the photogenic process would be labeled a photogram, sun picture, or printing-out print, in which objects rest directly atop sensitized paper [FIG. 3]. Eventually, this would lead to what we now consider the "positive" and "negative" processes in photography.

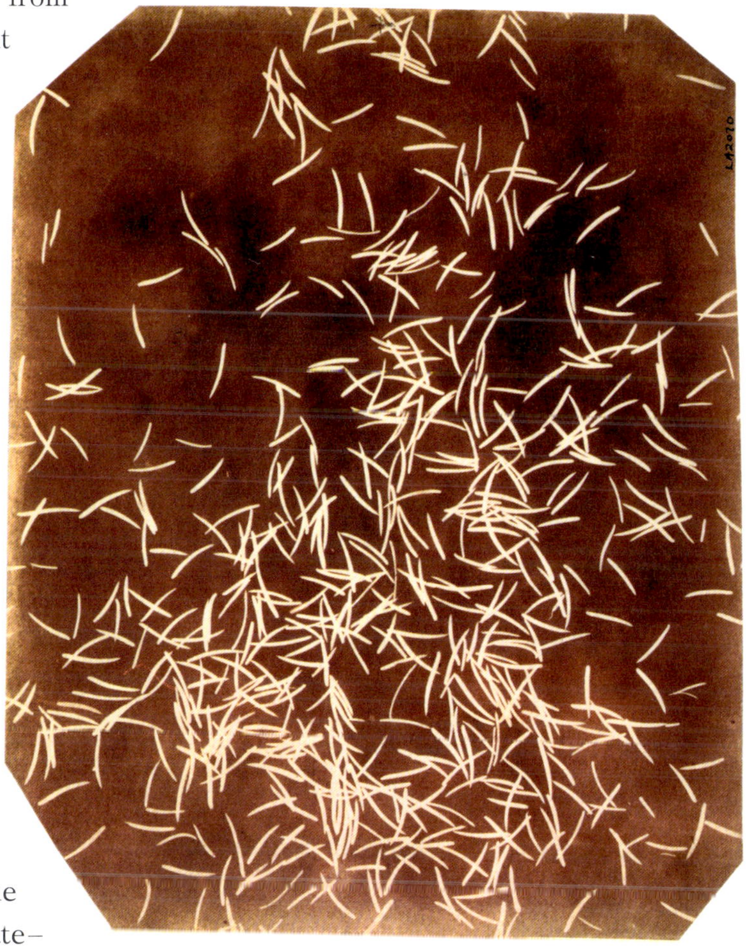

Ever the perfectionist, Talbot was still frustrated by his lack of progress and actually turned away from photography for four years, citing a "want of sufficient leisure for experiments" and a belief that "the clue was still wanting to this labyrinth of facts."[5] Talbot's lack of free time may have been caused by the birth of his first daughter, Ela, on April 25, 1835, and then of another, Rosamond, on March 16, 1837. He also remained active in the field of classics, publishing *Hermes, or Classical and Antiquarian Researches* in two volumes (1838 and 1839). A subsequent tome, *The Antiquity of the Book of Genesis: Illustrated by Some New Arguments* (1839), continued these interests in ancient history.

An announcement in early January 1839 grabbed Talbot's attention and inspired his return to photography. On January 7 Arago announced the invention by Daguerre of a metal plate—

FIG. 3

Needles of Spruce Fir, ca. 1839
Photogenic drawing negative
8⅞ × 7⁵⁄₁₆ in. (22.6 × 18.5 cm)
Fox Talbot Collection, The British Library, London

4   William Henry Fox Talbot, "Brief Historical Sketch of the Invention of the Art," in *The Pencil of Nature* (London: Longman, Brown, Green and Longmans, 1844–46; facsimile edition, New York: Da Capo Press, 1969), n.p.

5   Ibid.

based photographic system called the daguerreotype [FIG. 4]. The process, hailed by many for its clarity and quality, is generally considered the first to permanently fix an image. Talbot, perhaps upset that he had put aside his earlier photogenic experiments, scrambled to publish his own results in a paper entitled "Some Account of the Art of Photogenic Drawing, or the Process by Which Natural Objects May Be Made to Delineate Themselves without the Aid of the Artist's Pencil," which he read to the Royal Society on January 31.

Although competition likely played a role in the hastiness of Talbot's announcement, his next step was motivated by an entirely different impulse. On February 21, 1839, he delivered a more detailed paper on his discovery, which clearly outlined specifics such that others could replicate and improve upon his efforts. For Talbot, it was important that the photogenic process function flawlessly even if it meant someone else discovering a better way. Unlike Daguerre, Talbot did not initially seek remuneration for his invention because, as a true gentleman scientist, his reward was knowing that the process worked. In order for it to compete with the daguerreotype, though, Talbot had to solve the vexing problem of images on paper fading or darkening over time. For this, he relied on his knowledge of chemistry and his connections to other similarly inspired thinkers.

Sir John Herschel was, like Talbot, skilled in a variety of

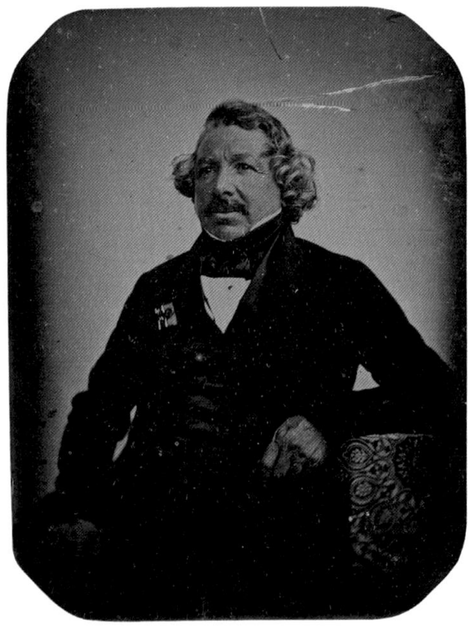

fields and equally captivated by the emerging photographic discoveries. His experiments, theories, and
terminology (he was the first to use the terms
"photograph" and "positive and negative")
proved essential to the advancement of the
medium [FIG. 5]. In close dialogue with
Talbot, Herschel discovered a means of fixing (a process he called "washing out" in
which unexposed silver compounds were
removed from the paper) that would allow
for more permanent recording of images.
Herschel was generous with his knowledge
and advice—he and Talbot were in close and
constant contact through letters and visits—
and this helped spur Talbot on. Eventually, in
1840, Talbot made his greatest leap in photography.

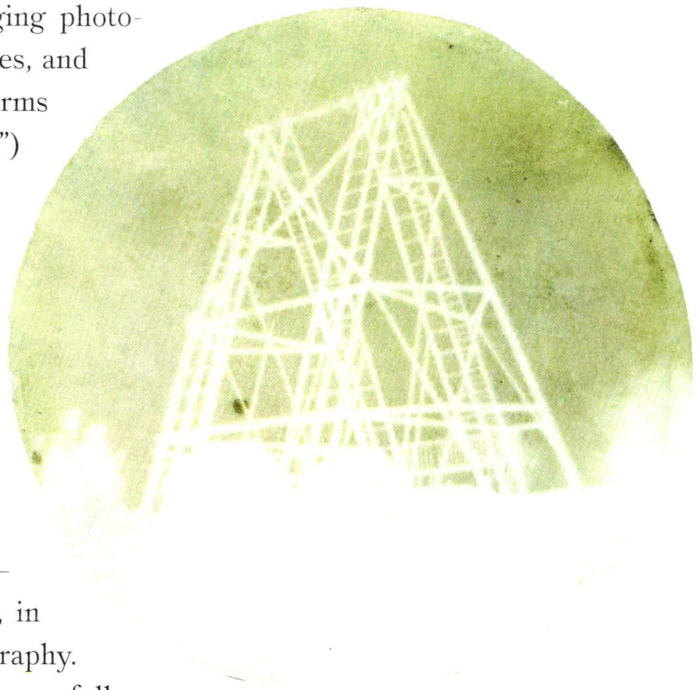

By September of that year, Talbot was fully
devoted to his new medium, which resulted in two successive
discoveries astonishingly made within a matter of days. On September 17,
he experimented with a process he called a "leucotype" in which he "fixed" a
direct-positive photograph using only hot water, rather than expensive
chemicals. Three days later, he tried out a new method of sensitizing paper
using gallic acid and silver nitrate (an idea first proposed by Herschel) that
resulted in much greater sensitivity. The process was one we now refer to as
"developing out," in which an image is captured on paper, but not revealed
until a later chemical application. This meant that instead of needing to
expose a piece of paper to light for many minutes or even hours, Talbot
could now expose a sheet in a few minutes or even seconds. Instead of photographing only still, inanimate objects, Talbot could now make pictures of
people and living things.

FIG. 5

Sir John Herschel
(British, 1792–1871)
*The Framework of Sir William
Herschel's Forty-Foot Telescope
at Slough*, autumn 1839
Photogenic drawing negative
3¹³⁄₁₆ in. (9.8 cm) diameter
The Museum of the History of
Science, Oxford, 1928-71
(Inventory #85037)

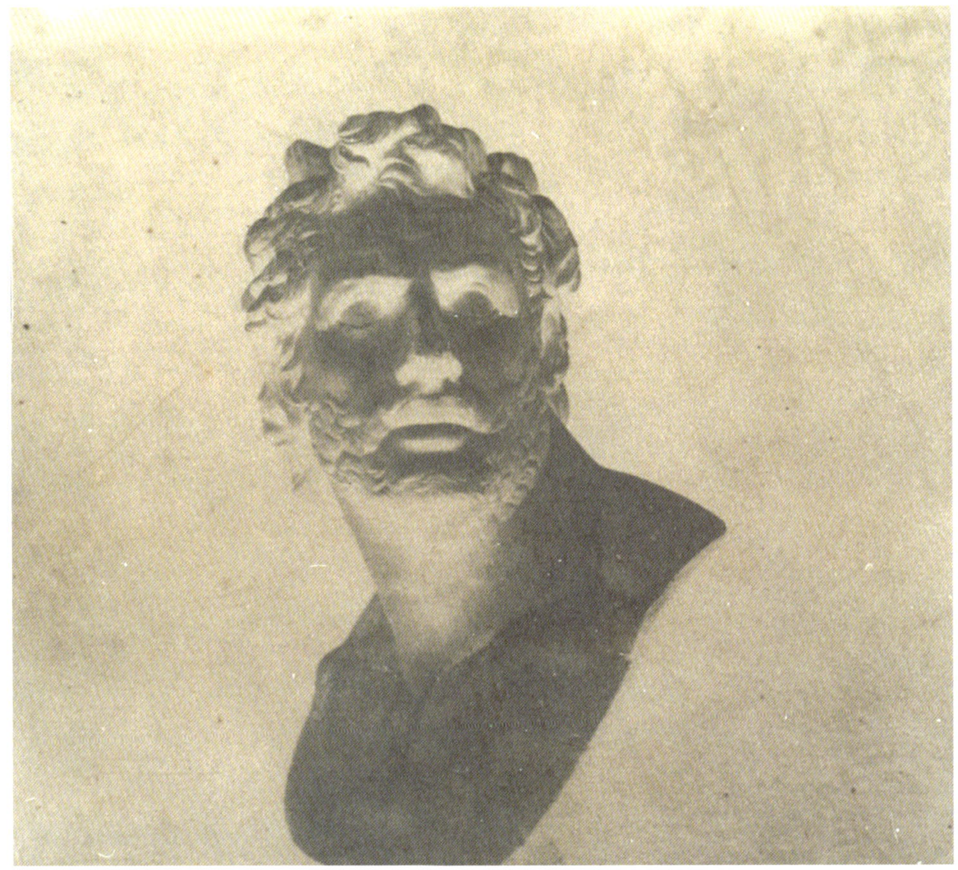

Talbot clearly relished this increased range of subjects. He graduated from using botanical specimens, lace, and paintings on glass to photographing the grounds of Lacock Abbey and his family and friends. In addition to serving as experiments, these photographs could also be given to others as souvenirs of an event. Eventually, he desired to branch out even more, finding his own environs "not particularly suited to the Artist" and offering "no great variety of subjects."[6] Talbot sought to push the boundaries of this new invention and, significantly, this gentleman of science thought of himself as "the Artist" best suited for that task.

Sensing the almost limitless potential of this new process that allowed for shorter exposures in dim lighting situations, Talbot would patent it as the "calotype" in 1841. The term, derived from the Greek *kalos* (beautiful) and *type* (impression), entailed creating a negative image on a sensitized sheet of paper [FIGS. 6, 7]. That paper was then put in direct contact with another sheet of light-sensitive paper and placed in the sun to create a new, positive image (page 77). Unlike the daguerreotype, which created a unique, singular image on a metal plate, Talbot's calotype could be duplicated endlessly, much in the modern sense of making prints from a negative; this made it highly suitable for printing and book making. Talbot had always believed his paper-based process would win out because of its relative economy and reproducibility, and the calotype seemed to prove him right.

Talbot understood the great potential for his new calotype process and was quick to publish his discovery (to avoid getting overtaken by Daguerre yet again), though hesitant to discuss specifics. Herschel wrote to Talbot, "I read your circular received this morning giving an account of the Kalotype [*sic*]. I always felt sure you would perfect your processes till they equaled or surpassed Daguerre's, but this is really magical. Surely you deal with the naughty one."[7] Even for someone as methodical and logical as Herschel, it seemed the only way Talbot could have obtained such rich and clear images was by dark magic.

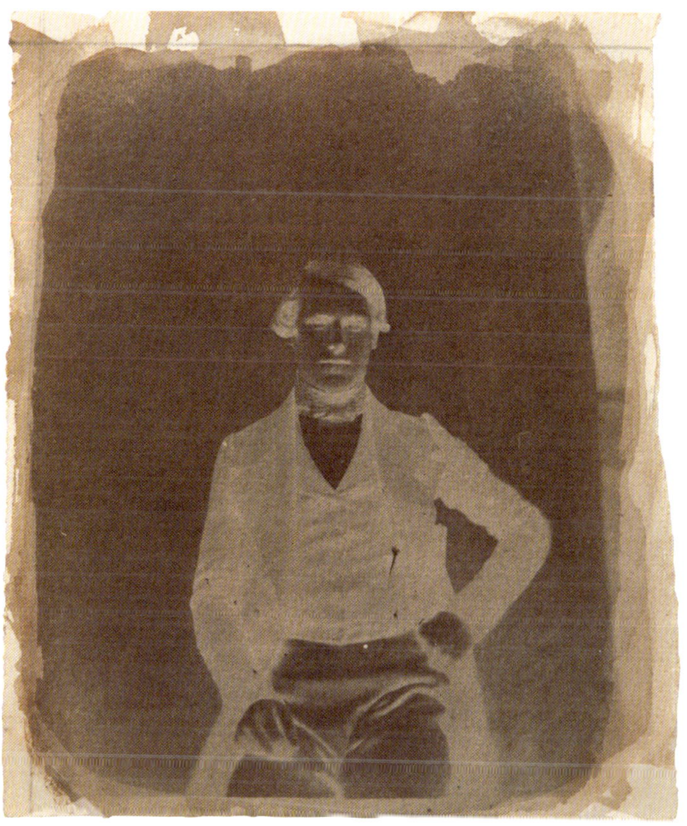

6   Talbot to Herschel, March 18, 1841,
     Royal Society, London; transcribed in
     Correspondence, Doc. No. 4218.

7   Herschel to Talbot, March 16, 1841,
     National Science & Media Museum,
     Bradford; transcribed in *Correspondence*, Doc. No. 4213.

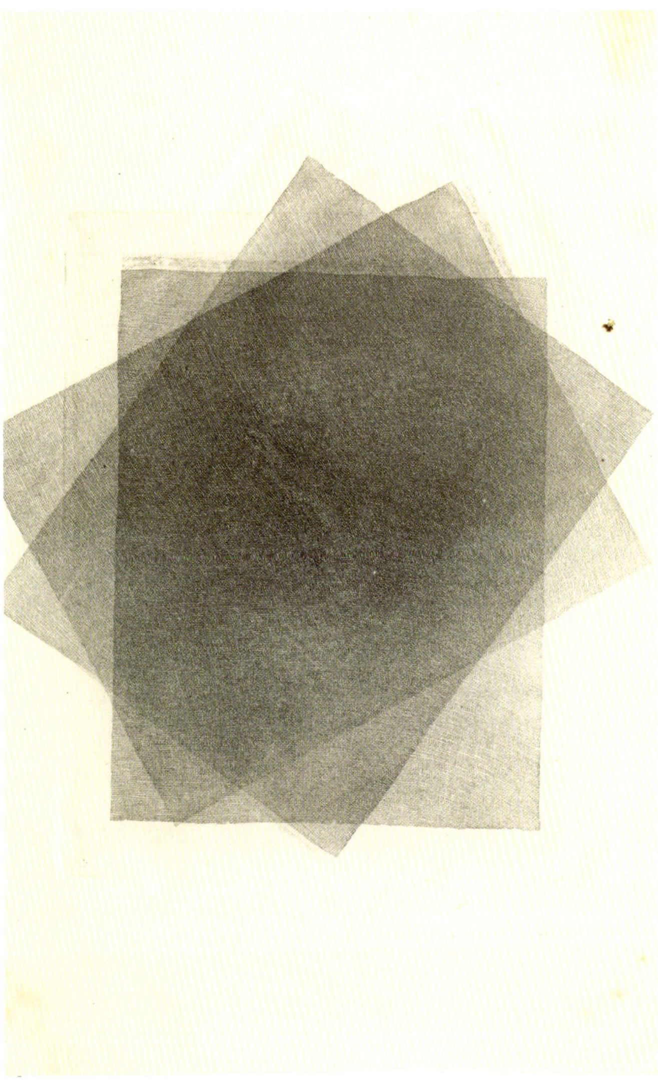

Three Sheets of Gauze, Crossed Obliquely, 1852–57
Photographic engraving
5¼ × 5 in. (13.3 × 12.7 cm)
(irregular) image; 8¹⁄₁₆ × 5¹⁄₁₆ in.
(20.5 × 12.8 cm) sheet
J. Paul Getty Museum, Los
Angeles, 2004.88.1

The logical direction that Talbot followed with his calotype was toward a photographic book, yet another innovation. Talbot backed his former valet, a Dutchman named Nicolaas Henneman, in setting up a printing business in Reading, England, in late 1843. The Reading Establishment offered a variety of services, including commissioned photographs and even lessons on how to make one's own calotypes. Primarily, it produced multiple copies of photographs. Scholar Larry J. Schaaf determined that the business made nearly eleven thousand prints in its first year alone.[8] A large portion of these were intended for Talbot's culminating accomplishment, the first commercially produced book illustrated with photographs, entitled *The Pencil of Nature* (1844–46).

Evidence of Talbot's and Henneman's unyielding passion and patience for photography lies in the fact that *The Pencil of Nature* took the better part of three years to produce. When finished, it comprised six parts containing twenty-four hand-printed photographs, each accompanied by Talbot's writings. There were approximately two hundred copies made of each of the six parts, and there was very little potential for financial reward.[9] For Talbot, the book was not about making money or receiving acclaim, but rather showcasing the exciting possibilities of this new medium and providing a platform to share these incredible discoveries.

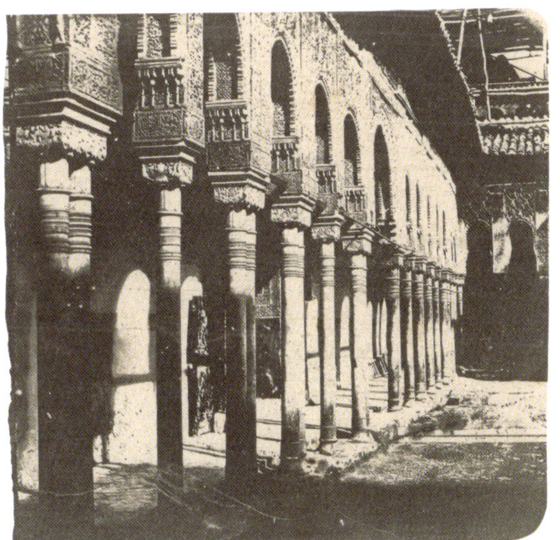

Never one to be satisfied with an unfinished product, Talbot continued to tinker with photographic processes. In 1852 and 1858, respectively, he patented two inventions related to the printing of images. He was working on photographs printed with ink rather than silver, as he came to believe, rightly so, that silver-based photography would forever be unstable and impermanent. Talbot's "photographic engraving" and "photoglyphic engraving" processes were intended to supplant the traditional photograph in print and would eventually lead to what we now call the photogravure process, which continues to be used today [FIGS. 8, 9].

Eventually, perhaps feeling that he could make greater contributions in other fields, Talbot moved on to different work for the last decade of his life. In the study of Assyriology, he was instrumental in helping translate several ancient cuneiform tablets and published forty-eight papers in *Transactions of the Society of Biblical Archaeology* and *Transactions and Records of the Past*.[10] His passion for knowledge did not cease and his need to work continued to the end. When Talbot died in his sleep in 1877, he had been working on a new appendix for Gaston Tissandier's *History and Handbook of Photography*.[11] Despite pursuing other fields to satisfy his desire to learn, Talbot never lost interest in the promise of photography.

19

8   Larry J. Schaaf, *Out of the Shadows: Herschel, Talbot, and the Invention of Photography* (New Haven: Yale University Press, 1992), 140.

9   Gail Buckland, *Fox Talbot and the Invention of Photography* (Boston: David R. Godine, 1980), 83.

10   Michael Gray, Arthur Ollman, and Carol McCusker, *First Photographs: William Henry Fox Talbot and the Birth of Photography* (New York: Powerhouse Books, 2002), 131.

11   Ibid.

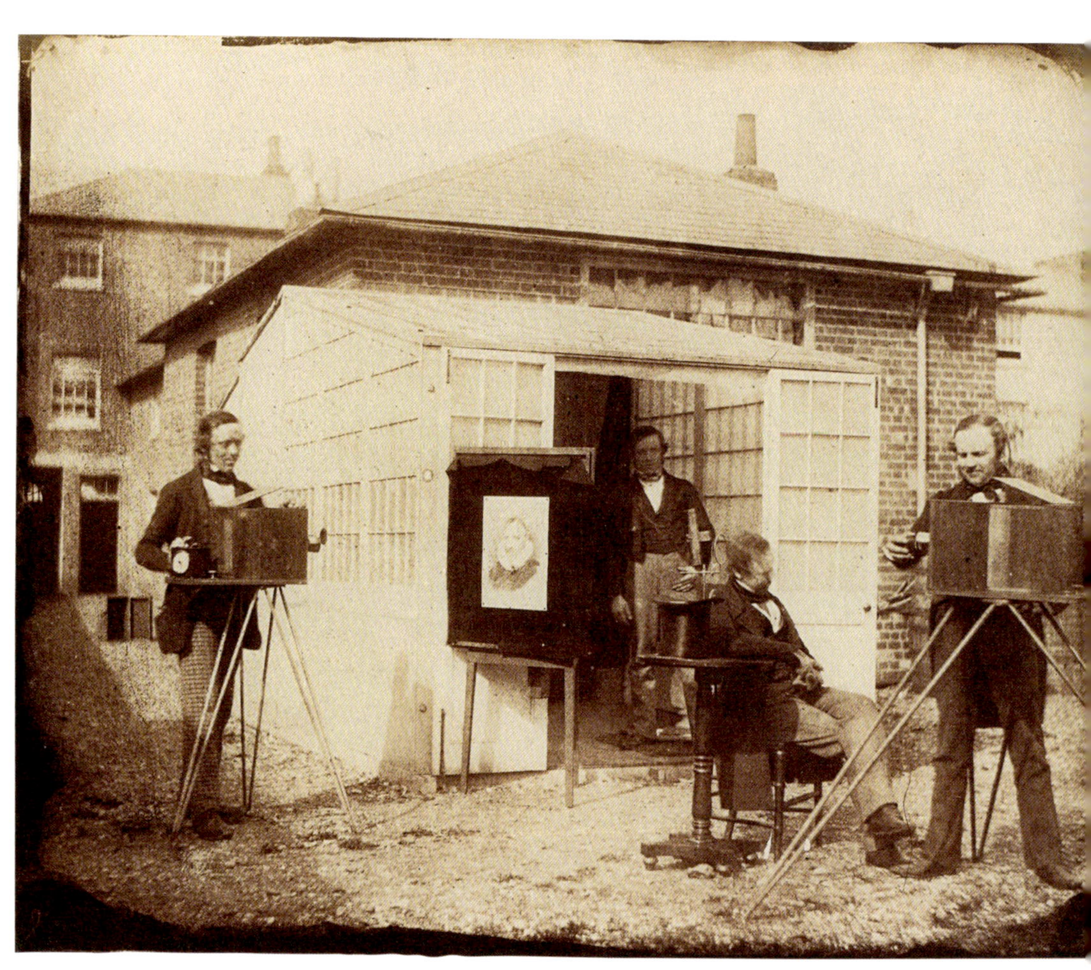

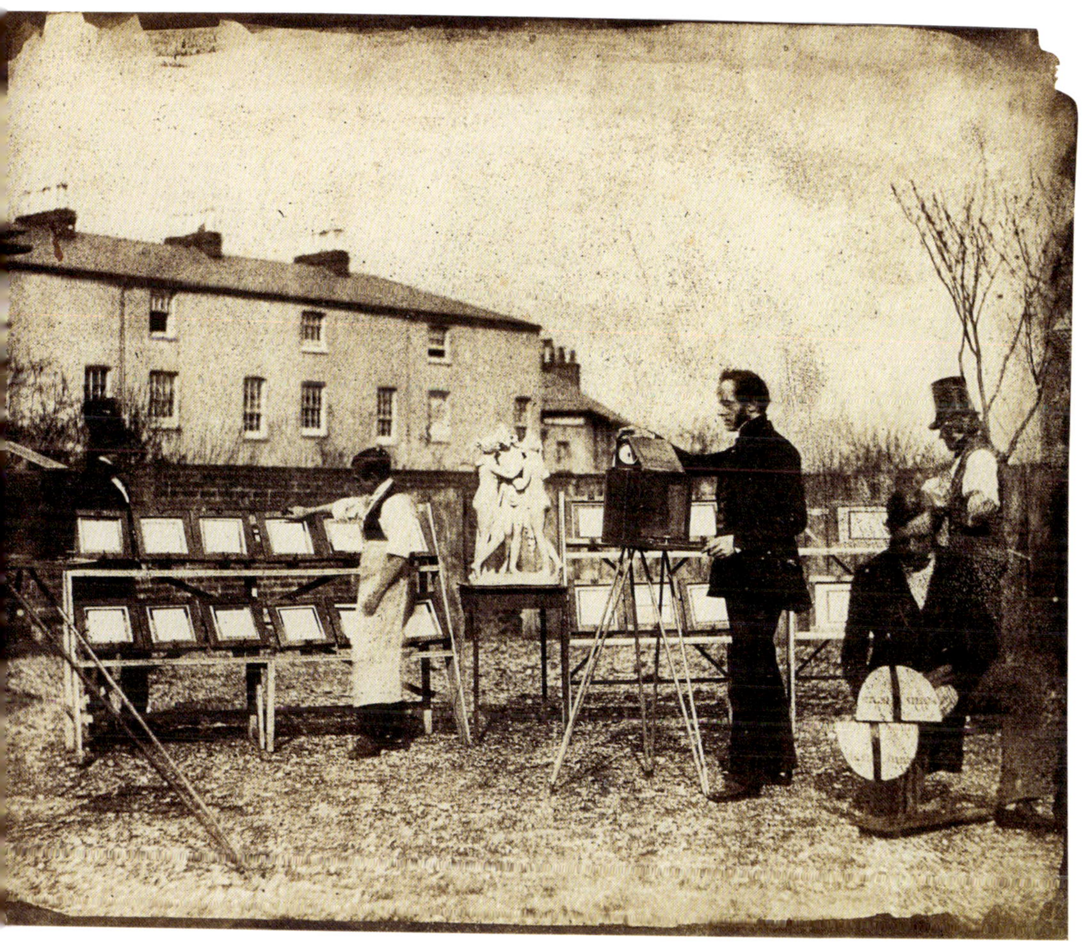

Attributed to William Henry
Fox Talbot (British, 1800–1877)
and Nicolaas Henneman
(Dutch, 1813–1898)
The Reading Establishment, 1846
Salted paper prints from paper
negatives
Left image: 7⁵⁄₁₆ × 8¹³⁄₁₆ in. (18.6 ×
22.4 cm); right image: 7⅛ × 8¹¹⁄₁₆
in. (18.1 × 22 cm); overall sheet:
7¹³⁄₁₆ × 19⁵⁄₁₆ in. (19.9 × 49.1 cm)
The Metropolitan Museum of Art,
New York, Gilman Collection,
Gift of The Howard Gilman
Foundation, 2005. 2005.100.
171.1, .2

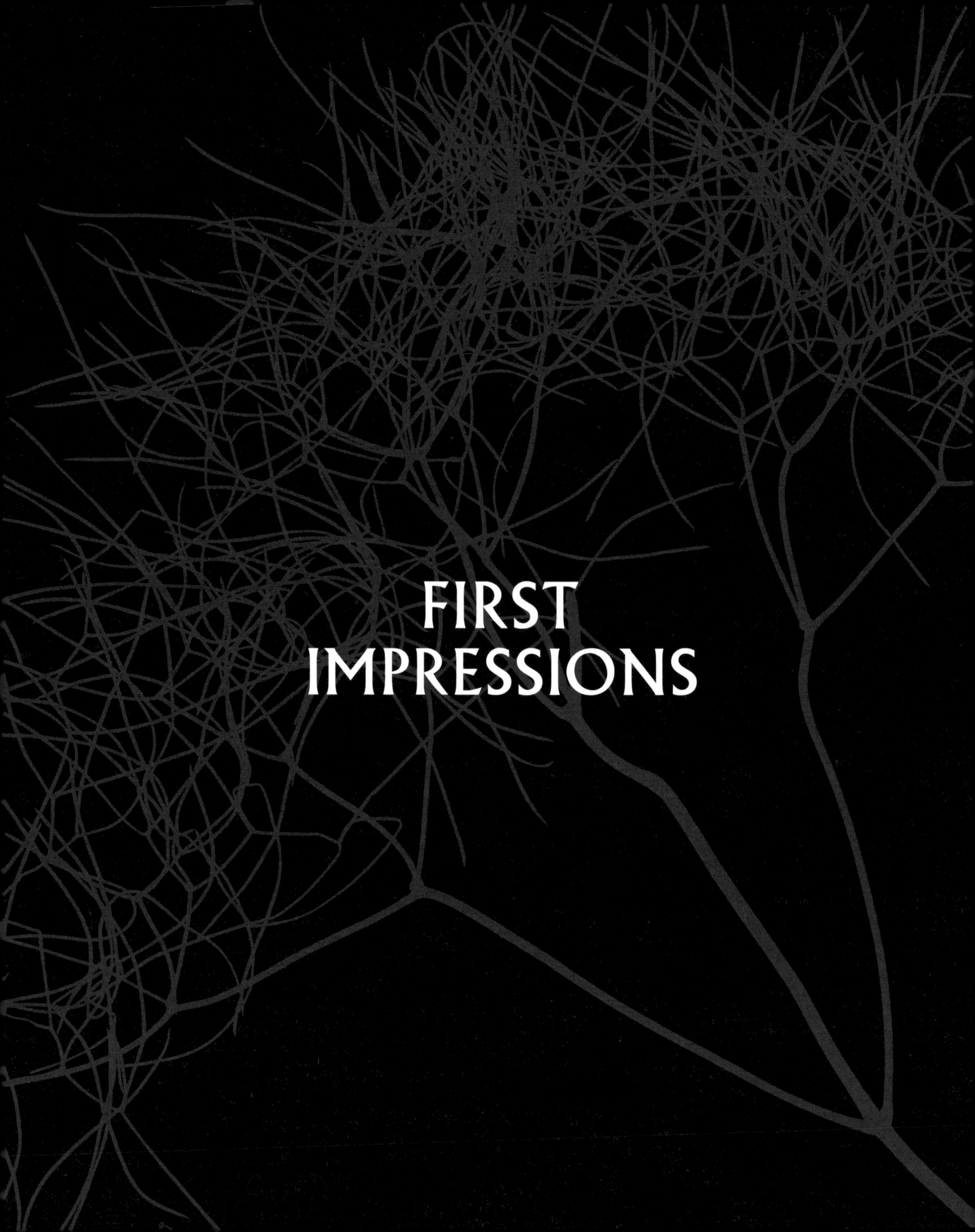

FIRST
IMPRESSIONS

In October 1833 William Henry Fox Talbot found himself on the shores of Lake Como in Italy, introducing his new wife, Constance, to the joys of the Grand Tour. She and other family members were happily sketching away, preserving their reactions and memories on drawing paper—everybody, that is, except for Talbot. As accomplished as he was in so many fields, he simply could not draw. Turning to technology, he tried his hand with a drawing instrument he had carried along on his travels for years, the camera lucida. But, as Talbot later noted, "when the eye was removed from the prism—in which all looked beautiful—I found that the faithless pencil had only left traces on the paper melancholy to behold."[1] Talbot had no idea how to reduce the complex three-dimensional, colorful world into monochromatic lines on two-dimensional paper. He then recalled his use of the camera obscura, a centuries-old artist's device that projected an image onto drawing paper, and became convinced that it should be possible to "imprint" images on paper. The following spring, back at his home of Lacock Abbey in Wiltshire, Talbot harnessed light-sensitive silver salts to obtain "distinct and very pleasing images of such things as leaves, lace, and other flat objects of complicated forms and outlines, by exposing them to the light of the sun."[2]

Establishing the goal of having Nature be his drawing mistress, Talbot zeroed in on a precise balance of chemistry. He first coated plain writing paper with a solution of table salt, dried it, and then brushed this over with a solution of silver nitrate. Light-sensitive silver chloride was precipitated and trapped within the surface fibers of the paper. Flat objects such as leaves or lace were then sandwiched under glass in contact with this paper and brought out into the daylight. Within minutes the areas of the paper not protected by the object were darkened by solar energy reducing the silver chloride to minute particles of metallic silver. The protected areas remained paper white. Once the image was visible, the paper was brought back indoors and fixed with chemicals to make it resist the further action of light.

In his private notebook in 1834, Talbot called these images "sciagraphs," referring to the theatrical practice of depicting an object through its shadow, a good indication of how he initially perceived what had been created. However, when he announced this process to the public in January 1839, he used the term "photogenic drawing." These unique primal images, beautiful in themselves, injected two critical elements into photography. Perhaps the most important was the use of paper, a familiar medium and one that would eventually merge the technique of photography with the world of books. Although he didn't put it into practice immediately, Talbot also grasped the concept that the inverted tones of these images could be copied onto additional sheets of sensitive paper, reversing them back. These negatives, as they later came to be known, allowed the production of precisely matching multiples. —LJS

1   William Henry Fox Talbot, "Brief Historical Sketch of the Invention of the Art," in *The Pencil of Nature* (London: Longman, Brown, Green and Longmans, 1844–46), n.p.

2   Ibid.

Buckler Fern, ca. 1839

Photogenic drawing negative

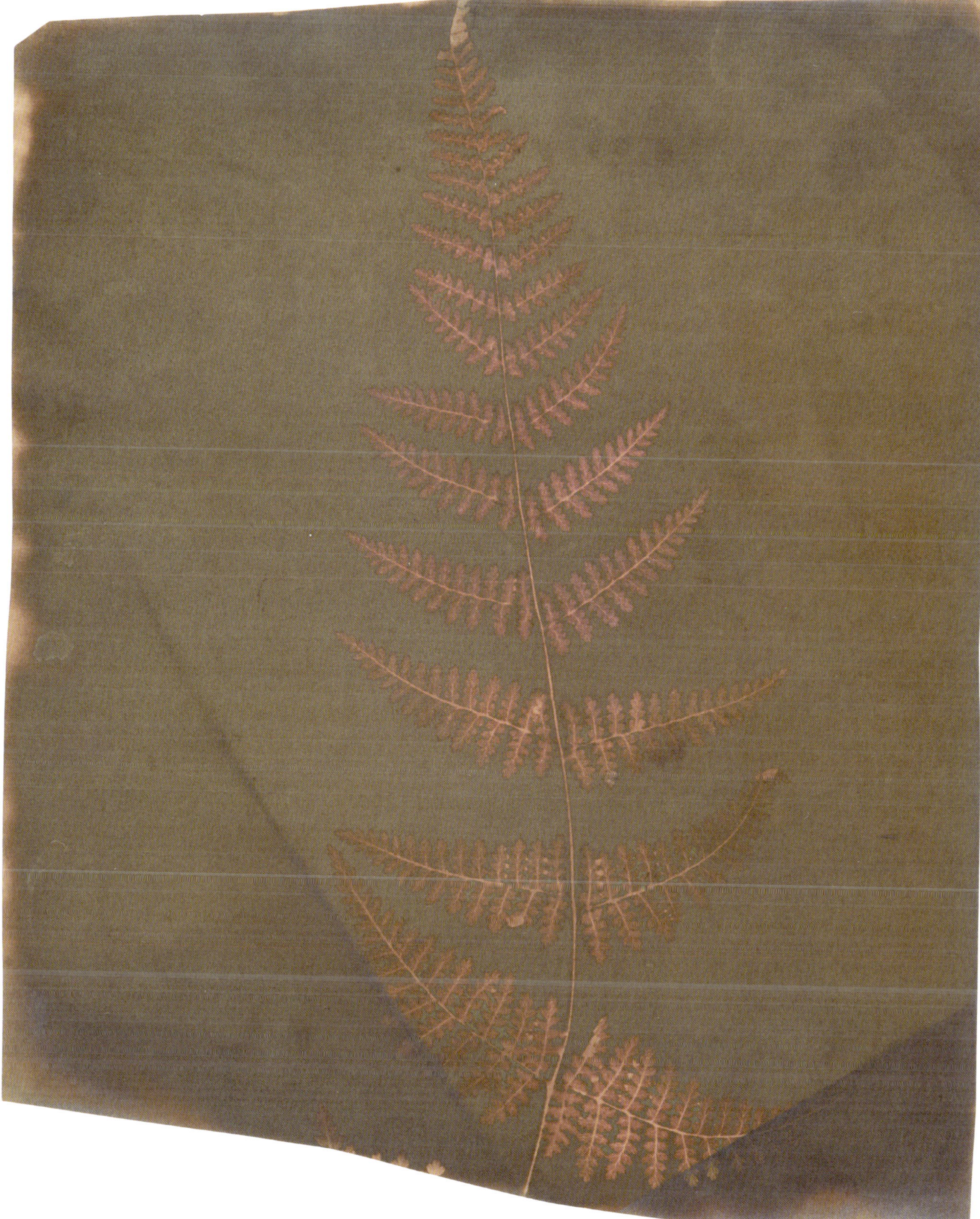

Leaves and Flowers of a Plant, ca. 1839

Photogenic drawing negative

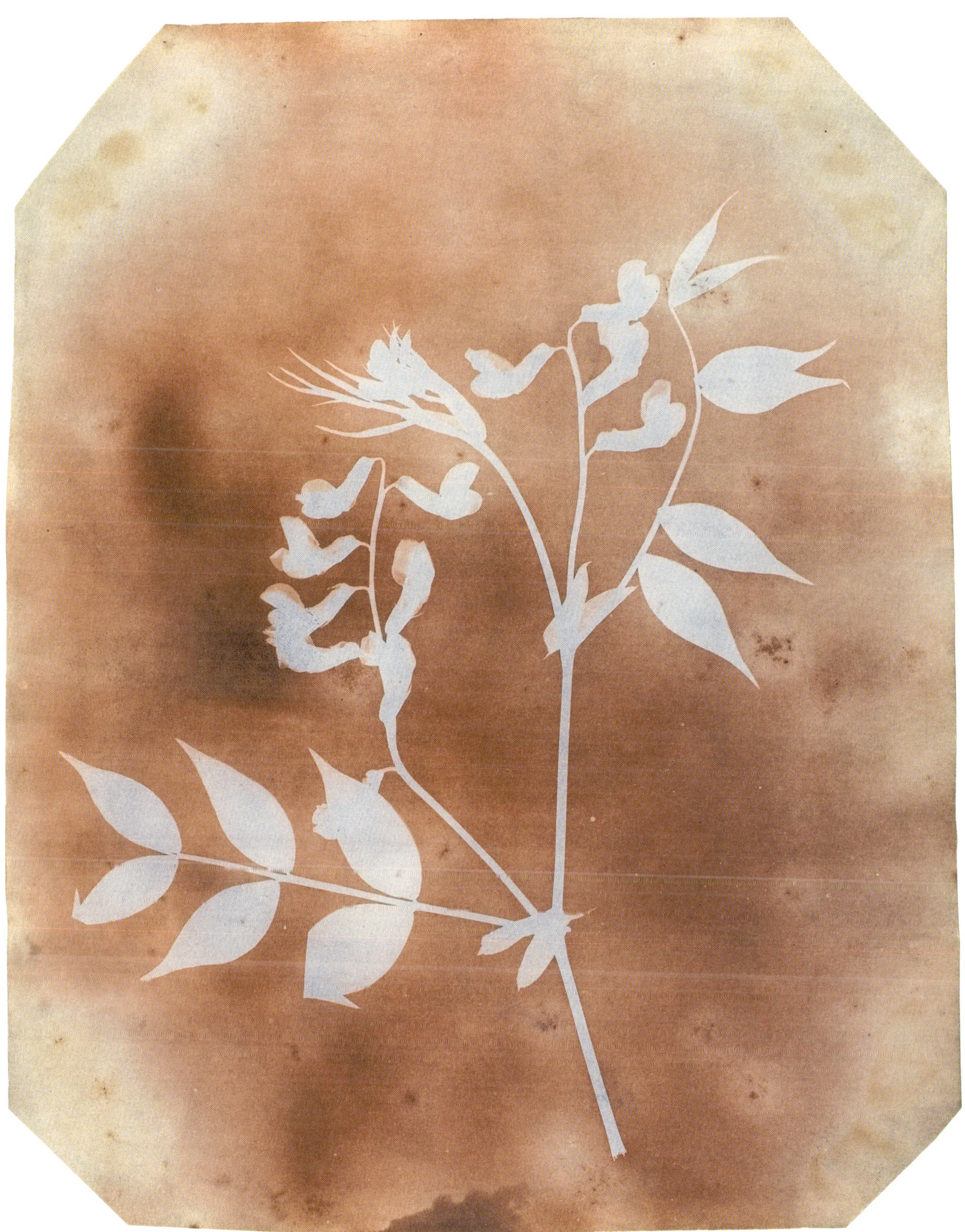

Wild Fennel, 1841–42

Salted paper print

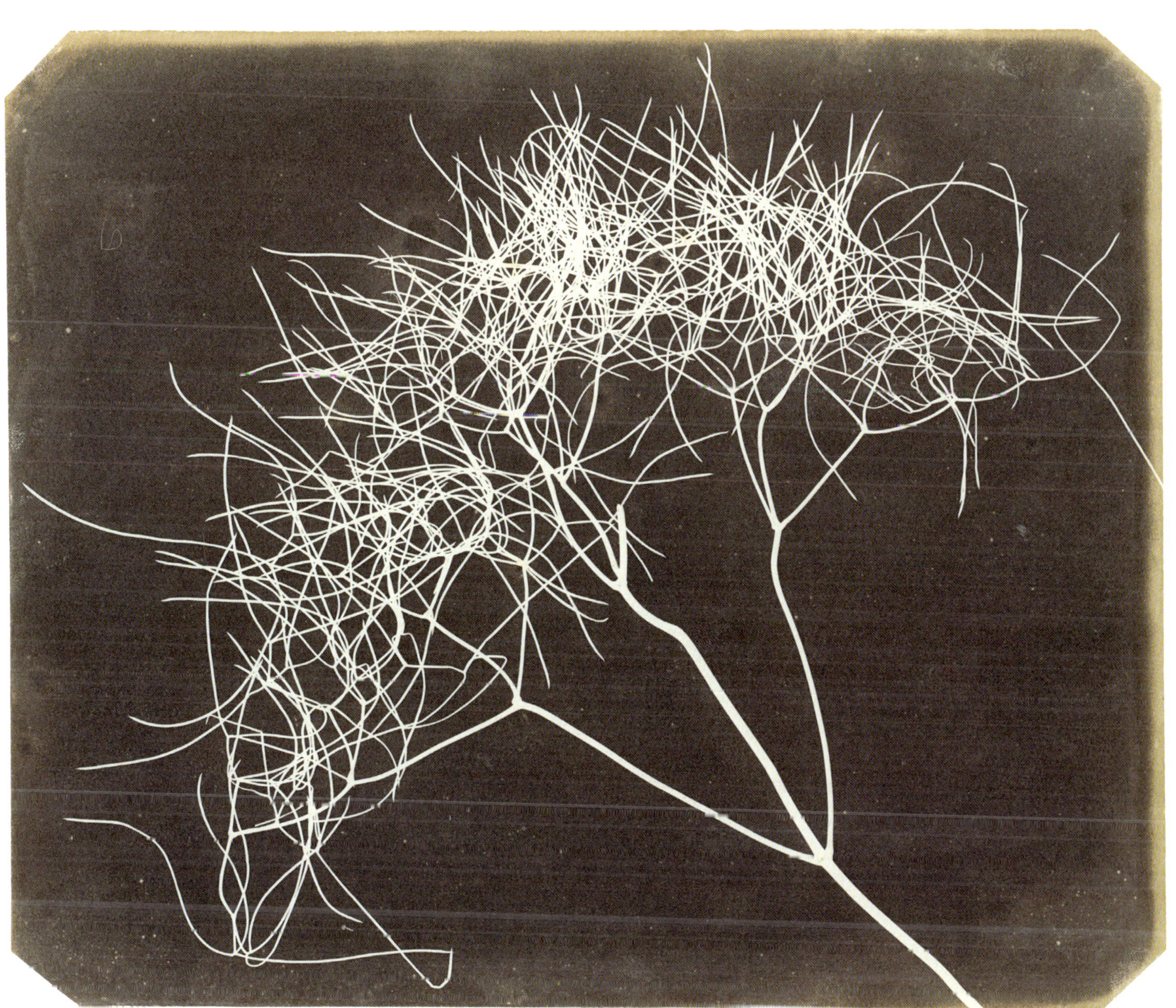

Attributed to Nicolaas Henneman

Black Cherry Leaves, mid–1840s

Photogenic drawing negative

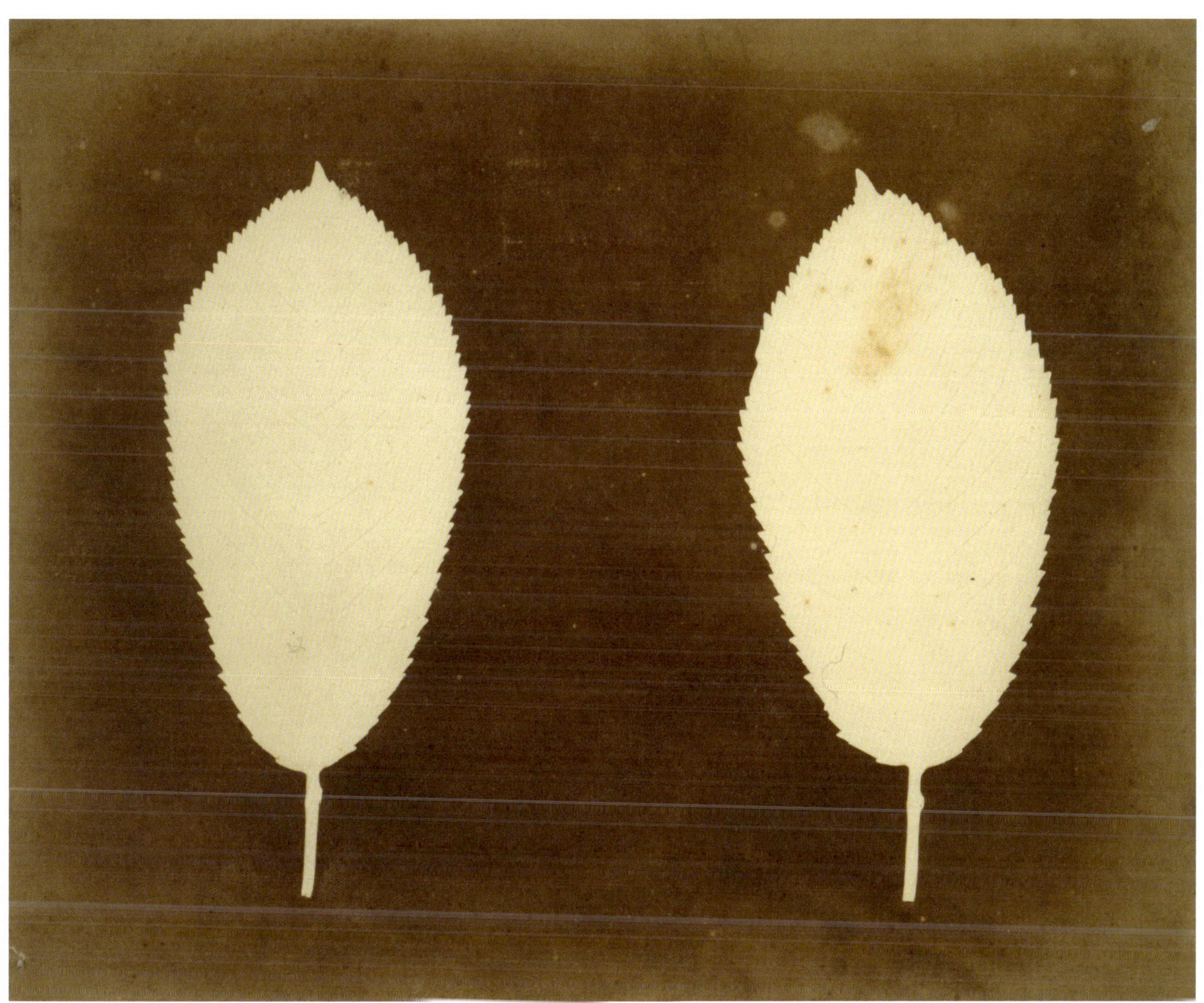

Lace, early 1840s

Salted paper print from a photogenic drawing negative

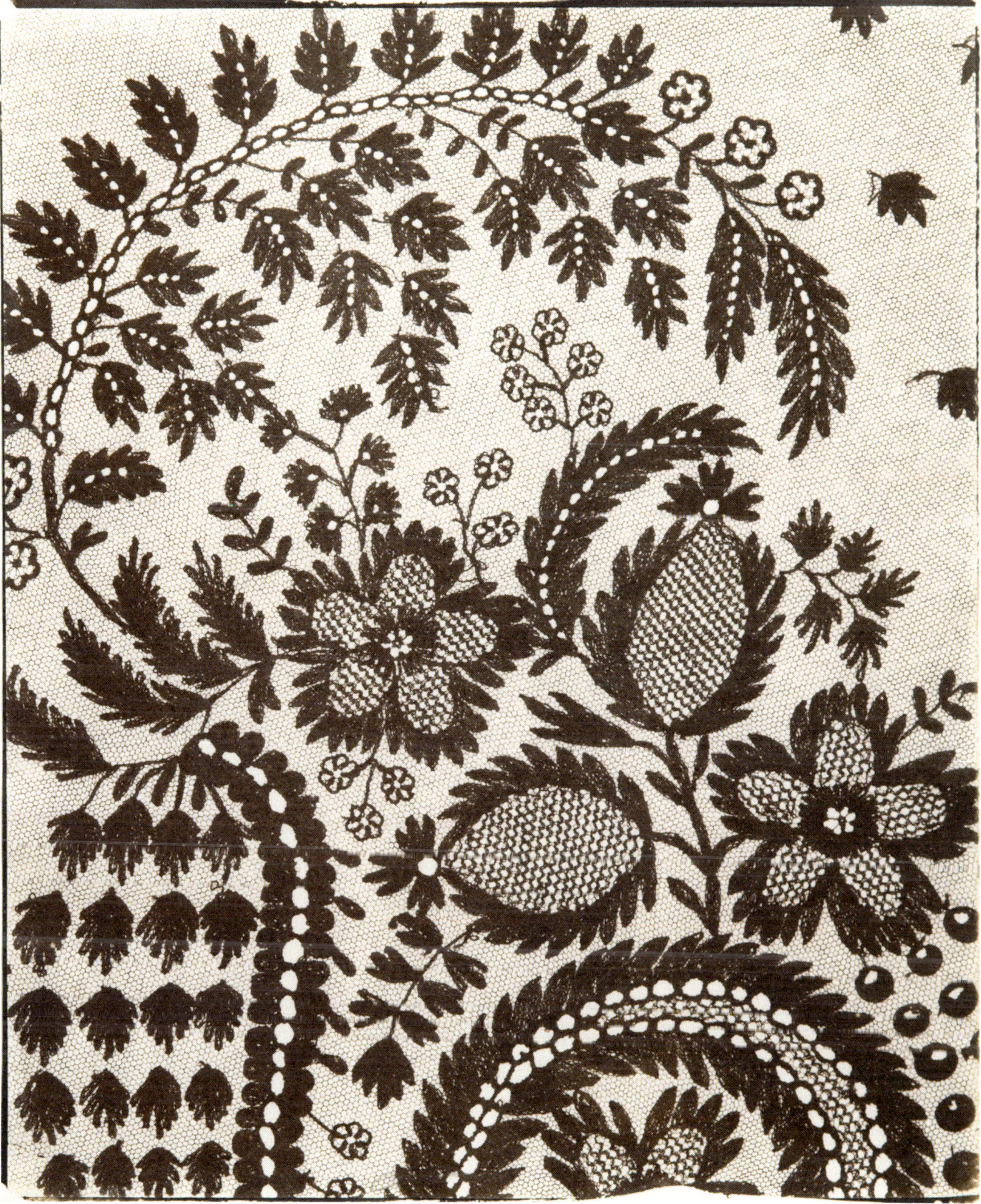

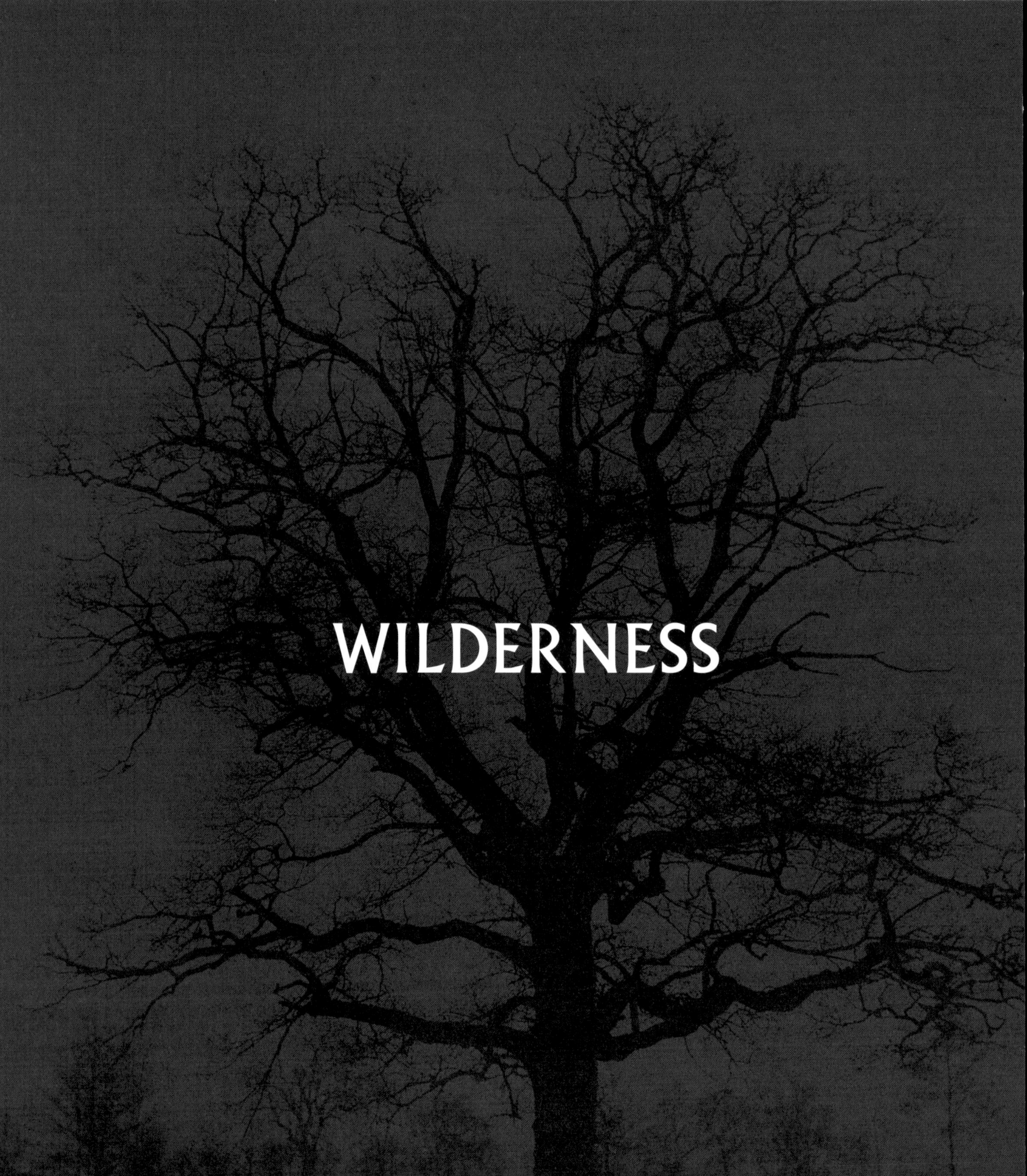

WILDERNESS

Throughout his long life, Talbot stood in awe of Nature. He was not an overtly religious man but more a scientist who understood and yet still marveled at the physical processes through which Nature exercised her powers.

But sometimes Nature chose to retain some mystique. Talbot's photographic processes naturally produced various colors, sometimes identifiable by the specific chemistry involved, sometimes puzzling. In his earliest work the chemistry yielded mostly lavender and yellowish colors. By the 1840s a range of browns became most common. These were not sepia toned but instead resulted from the physical characteristics of the minute silver clusters that composed the visible image. Microscopic, they varied in shape, surface texture, and spacing, reflecting and refracting the light that fell on them and bouncing back selective wavelengths. Butterfly wings work the same way; they actually have no color, but their cellular structure modulates the wavelengths of light, presenting our eyes with colors.

One of the most extraordinary of the tints that Talbot's processes produced is the rare fiery red tone of his *Trees in Winter*. What led to its specific color is not presently known, but Talbot clearly understood the visual power of this almost demonic and certainly arresting print. It is the earliest photograph in this group and was made using his photogenic drawing paper, first to produce a negative and then another sheet on which to make this print. The energy of sunlight did all the work here, leading to long exposure times for both the negative and the print.

In September 1840 Talbot's continuing experiments revealed a most surprising result. Thinking that an experiment had failed, leaving the paper unaffected, he went away for a period and then returned to his laboratory. Magically, the formerly blank sheet was now impressed with a strong image. It did not take the analytical Talbot long to get over his surprise and to unravel the secret. He had added a chemical, gallic acid, which acted as a developer. Unknown to Talbot, his too-short exposure in the camera had produced an invisible latent image. The gallic acid acted as an amplifier, substituting chemistry for light and bringing the image to full visibility. His exposure times plummeted from tens of minutes to a few seconds, greatly increasing the range of his subject matter.

Calling this new negative process the calotype, Talbot set out to capture the scenes of nature that formerly had eluded him. At first these were familiar surroundings, of his own estate and those of his relatives, but in October 1844 he ventured into Scotland, guided by Sir Walter Scott's prose. Talbot's *Loch Katrine* is startlingly modern in its composition—four converging triangles of alternating tone strongly setting a mood appropriate to the "Lady of the Lake." —LJS

Trees in Winter, winter 1839–40

Salted paper print from a photogenic drawing negative

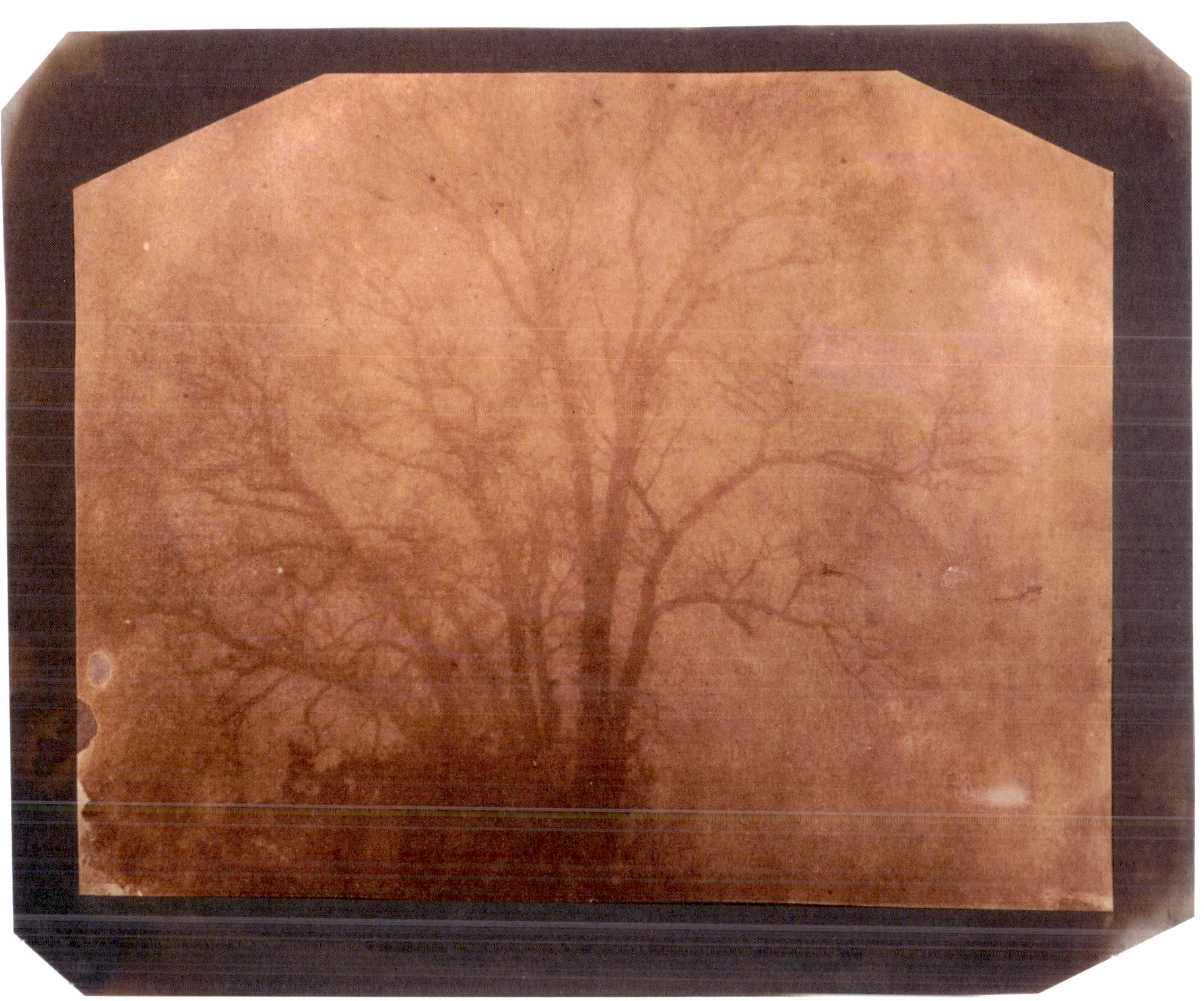

Scene in a Wood, summer 1842

Salted paper print from a calotype negative

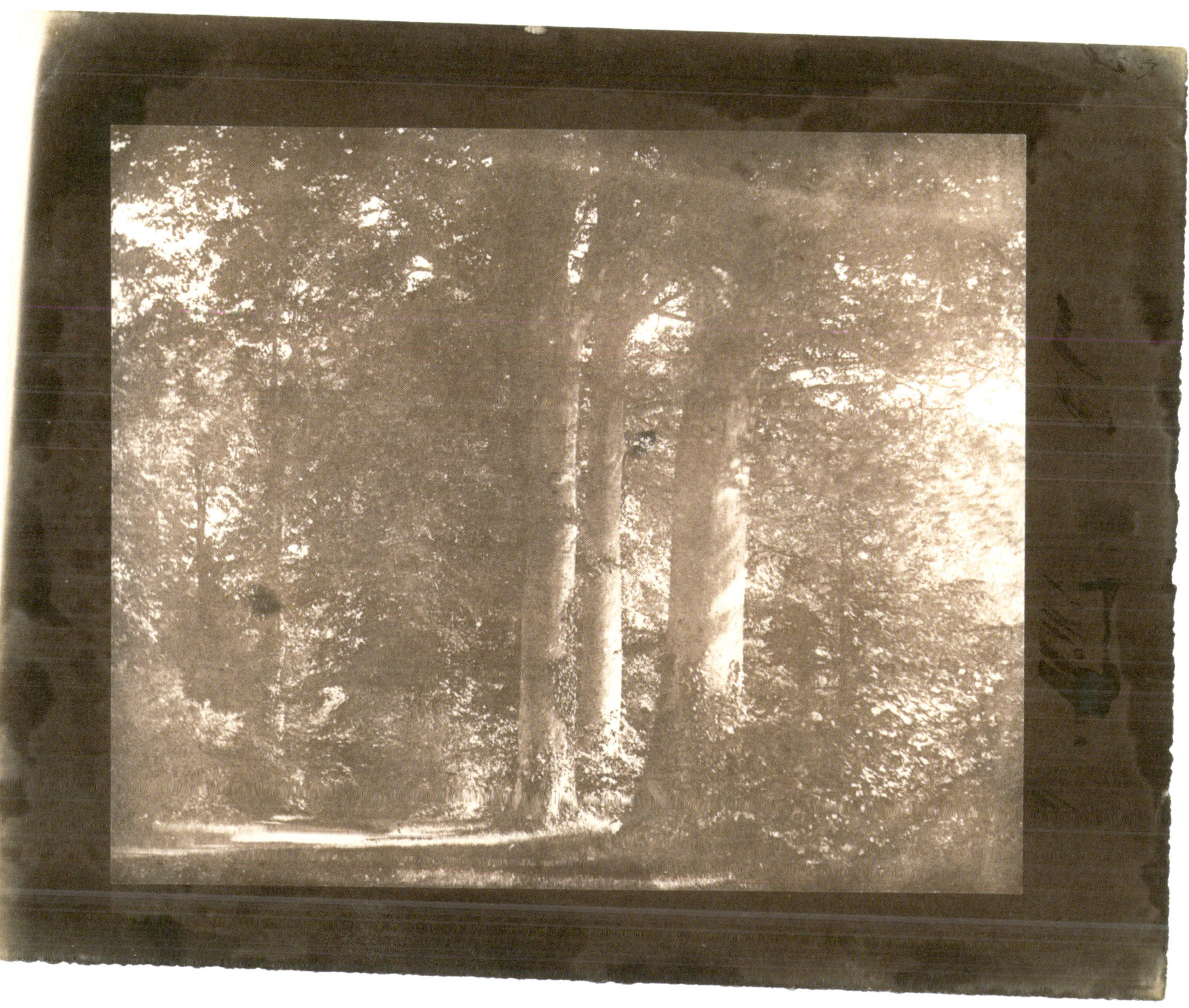

Oak Tree in Winter, 1842–43

Salted paper print from a calotype negative

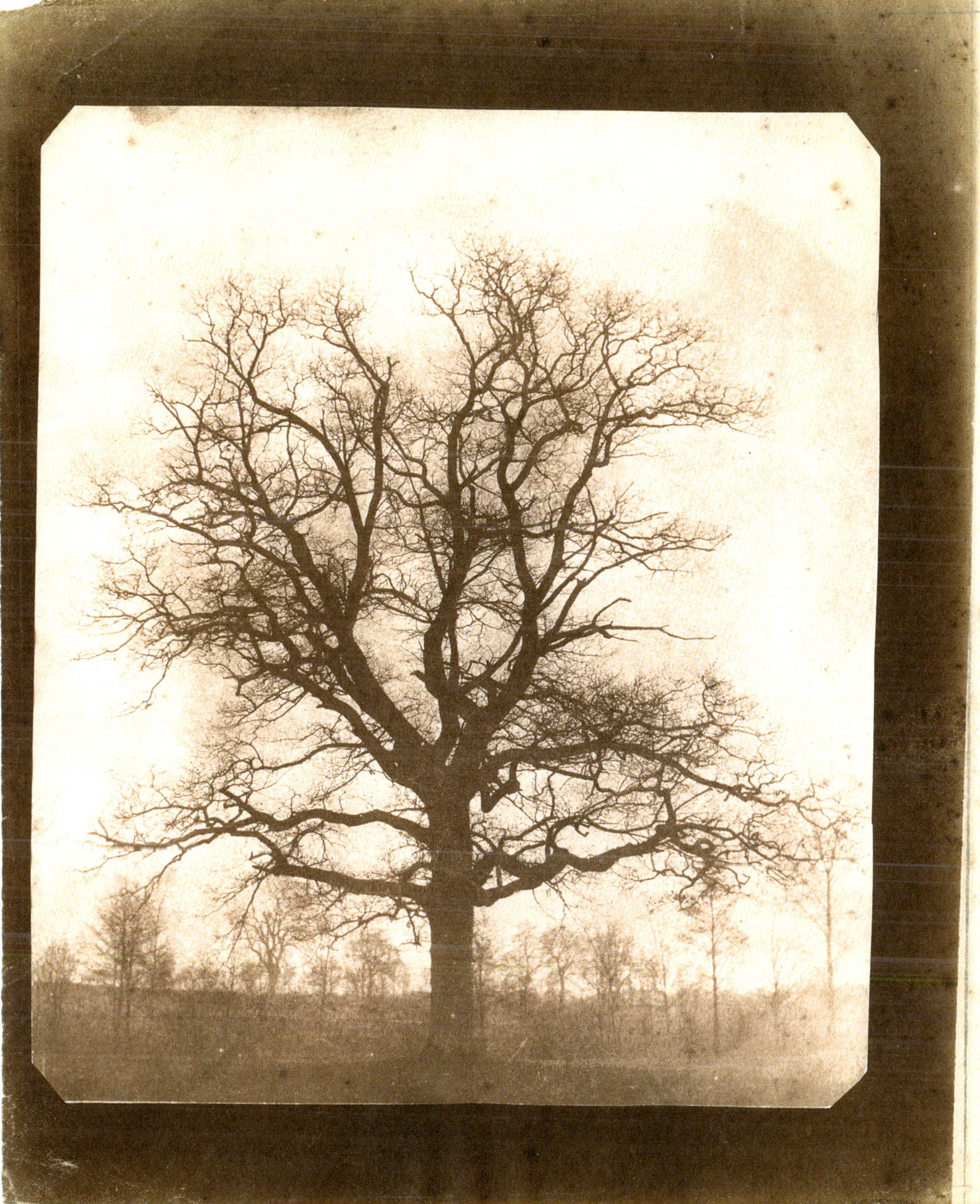

An Aged Red Cedar Tree in the Grounds of
Mount Edgcumbe, ca. 1845

Salted paper print, varnished, from a calotype negative

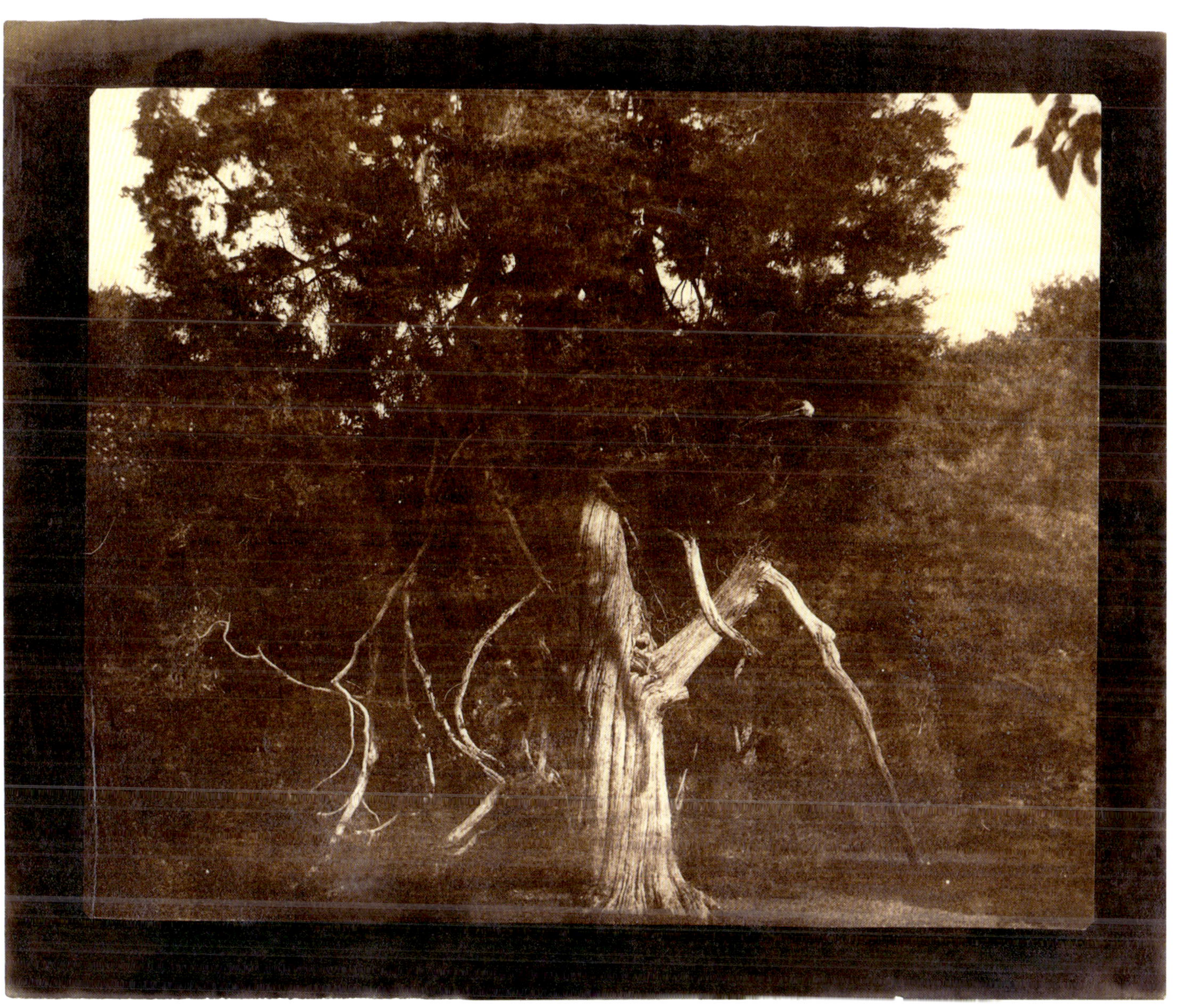

Loch Katrine, October 1844

Salted paper print from a calotype negative

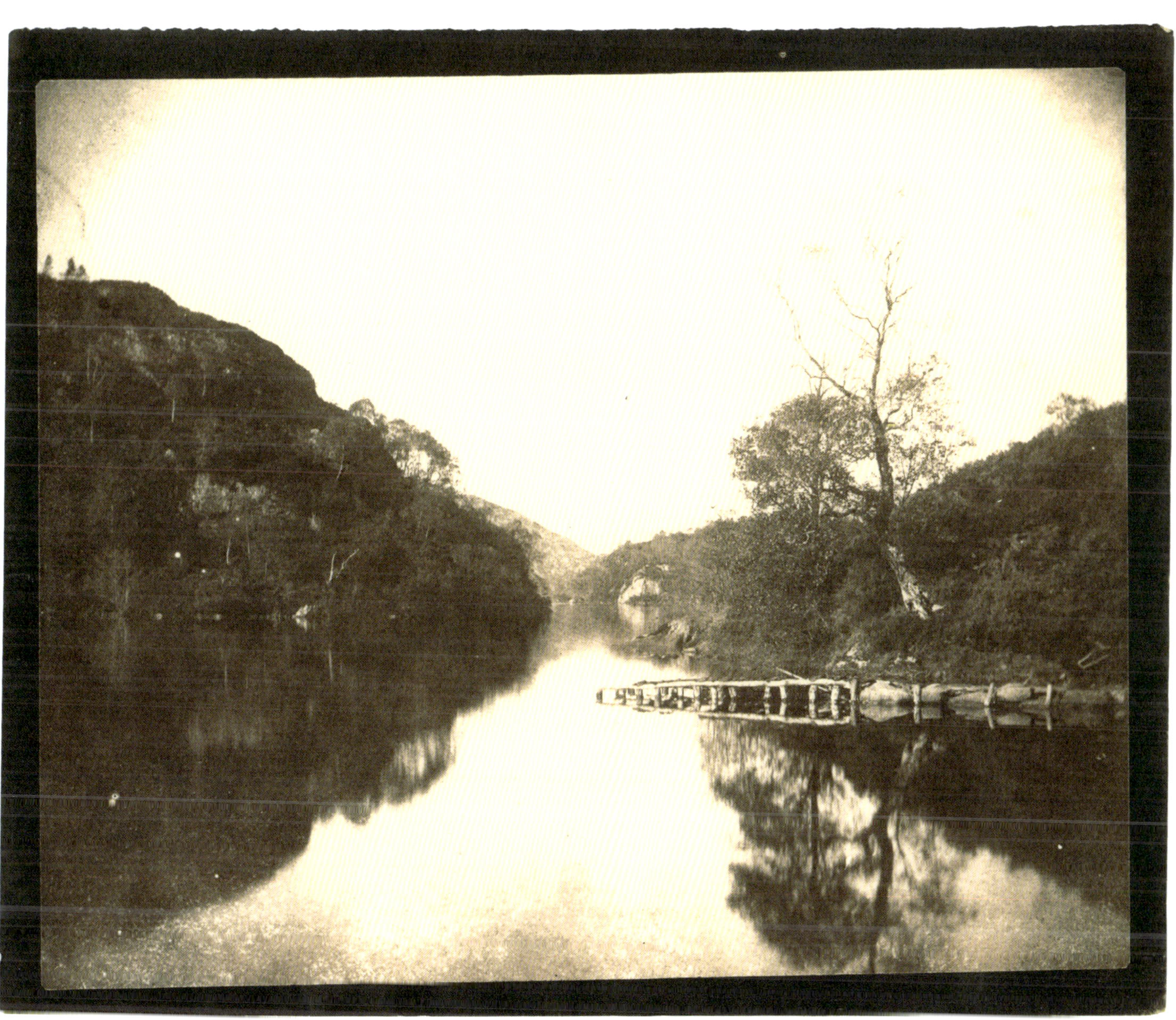

THE **INSPIRATION** OF LACOCK ABBEY

The medieval nunnery of Lacock Abbey in Wiltshire was Henry Talbot's rightful inheritance, but the death of his father just months after Henry's birth forced the letting of this ancestral home. He grew up in a succession of family houses, undoubtedly contributing to his wanderlust. At the age of eight, he wrote that he "cast up the number of miles I have travelled in my life to be 3219"—a highly unusual declaration for a child.[1] Talbot wasn't able to retake possession of the Abbey until he was twenty-seven years old. At first he didn't like it, but his formidable mother and muse, Lady Elisabeth Feilding, slowly won him over. Botany was one of Talbot's special passions, and the grounds and gardens of Lacock nurtured this interest. These plants supplied some of his earliest photographic subjects.

Most of Talbot's early photographic experiments were conducted at Lacock Abbey. There he had all of the resources of a country house, with numerous chemicals and containers seconded from the kitchen, an ample water supply, spare rooms to darken, and servants to assist him. As Talbot began to master the shorter exposure times of his calotype negatives, he found new subjects for his camera in and around the Abbey. Most startling was his turn to portraiture. When Queen Victoria appointed Talbot as the Sheriff of Wiltshire in 1840, photography was just ready to record the fine livery seen in *Footman at Carriage Door*. This pioneering negative was taken three weeks after his newly discovered calotype process made the relatively short three-minute exposure possible. Prior to that, even the most patient footman could not have withstood the ten times that long which photogenic drawing paper would have demanded. Less than four years after this, Talbot's mastery of photography was on full display in the highly detailed *Barouche in the North Courtyard of Lacock Abbey*.

In Talbot's day, his relatively well-off daughters might have expected to have their portrait painted once or twice in their lifetime. With their father's photography, their growth could be documented month by month, year by year, in a way that previous generations could never have dreamed of. A print showing his three daughters in the Cloisters at Lacock Abbey was cut in half long ago, possibly in preparation for mounting on album pages.

Within Talbot's work we sometimes find hints of his intellectual and aesthetic growth. The 1841 *Soliloquy of the Broom*, titled by Lady Elisabeth, is the earliest known attempt at what was to become his most famous and widely reproduced photograph, *The Open Door*, taken in 1844. In this early iteration, Talbot understood that he was onto a great image idea, and he repeatedly tried out various arrangements of the broom, its shadow, and the space of the stable room.

By 1845 Talbot began taking fewer photographs himself and encouraged others to advance the art. Although staged at Lacock Abbey, possibly with the collaboration of Talbot, *The Fruit Sellers* was probably directed and taken by his friend the Reverend Calvert R. Jones, a watercolorist and daguerreotypist who had become fully enamored of the calotype. —LJS

1   Entry for June 22, 1808, *William Henry Fox Talbot's Journal, 1806, 1807, 1808, 1809, 1810, 1811*; The British Library, London.

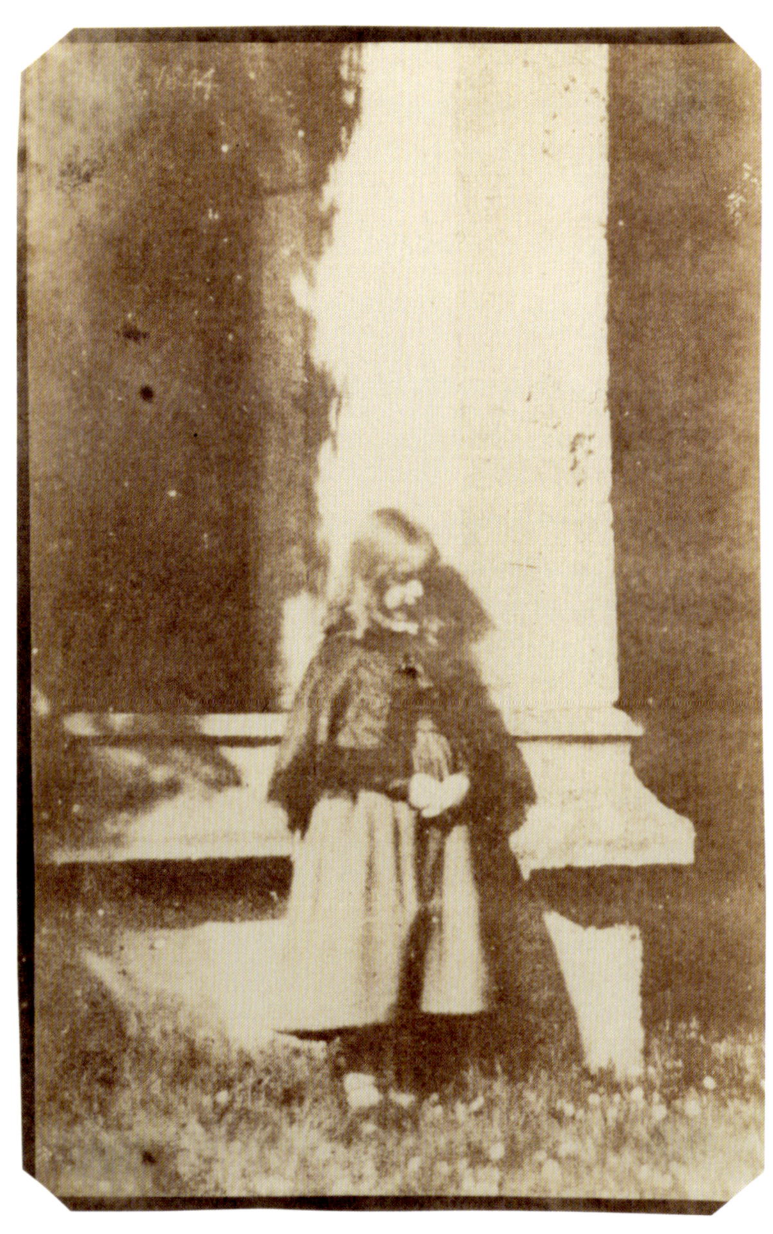

Rosamond Talbot in the Cloisters at
Lacock Abbey, April 1844

Left half of a salted paper print from a calotype negative

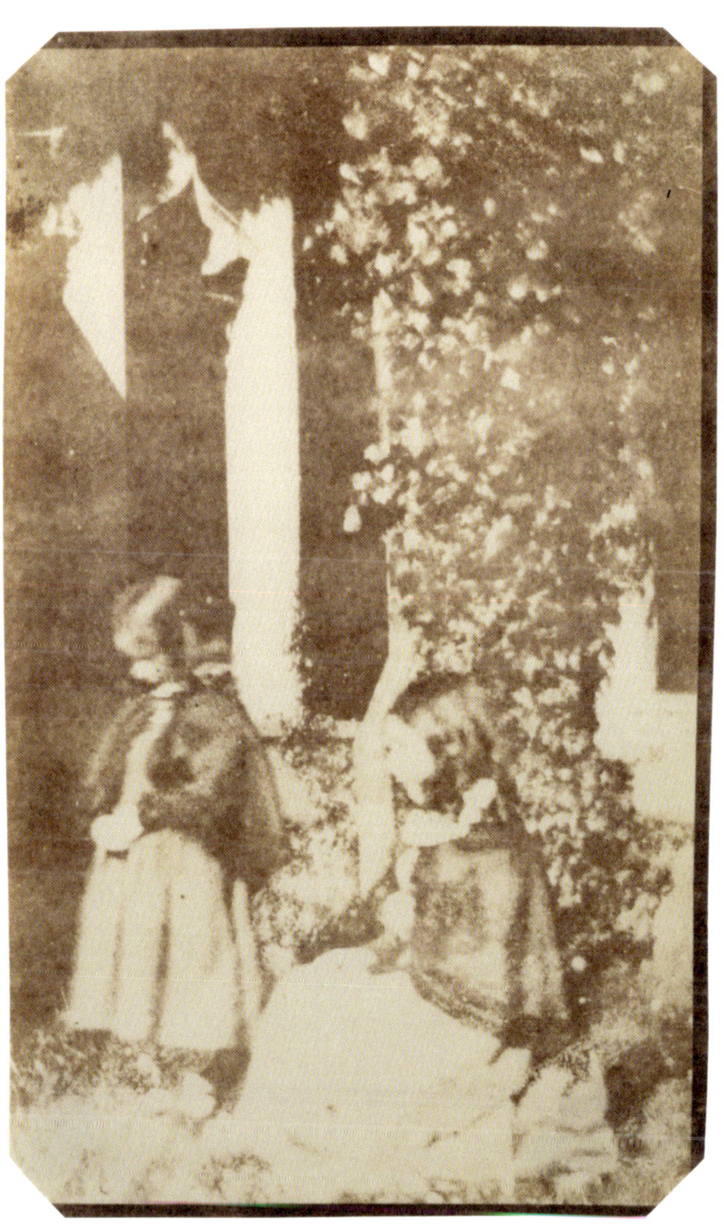

Matilda and Ela Talbot in the Cloisters at
Lacock Abbey, April 1844

Right half of a salted paper print from a calotype negative

A Barouche in the North Courtyard of
Lacock Abbey, April 1844

Salted paper print from a calotype negative

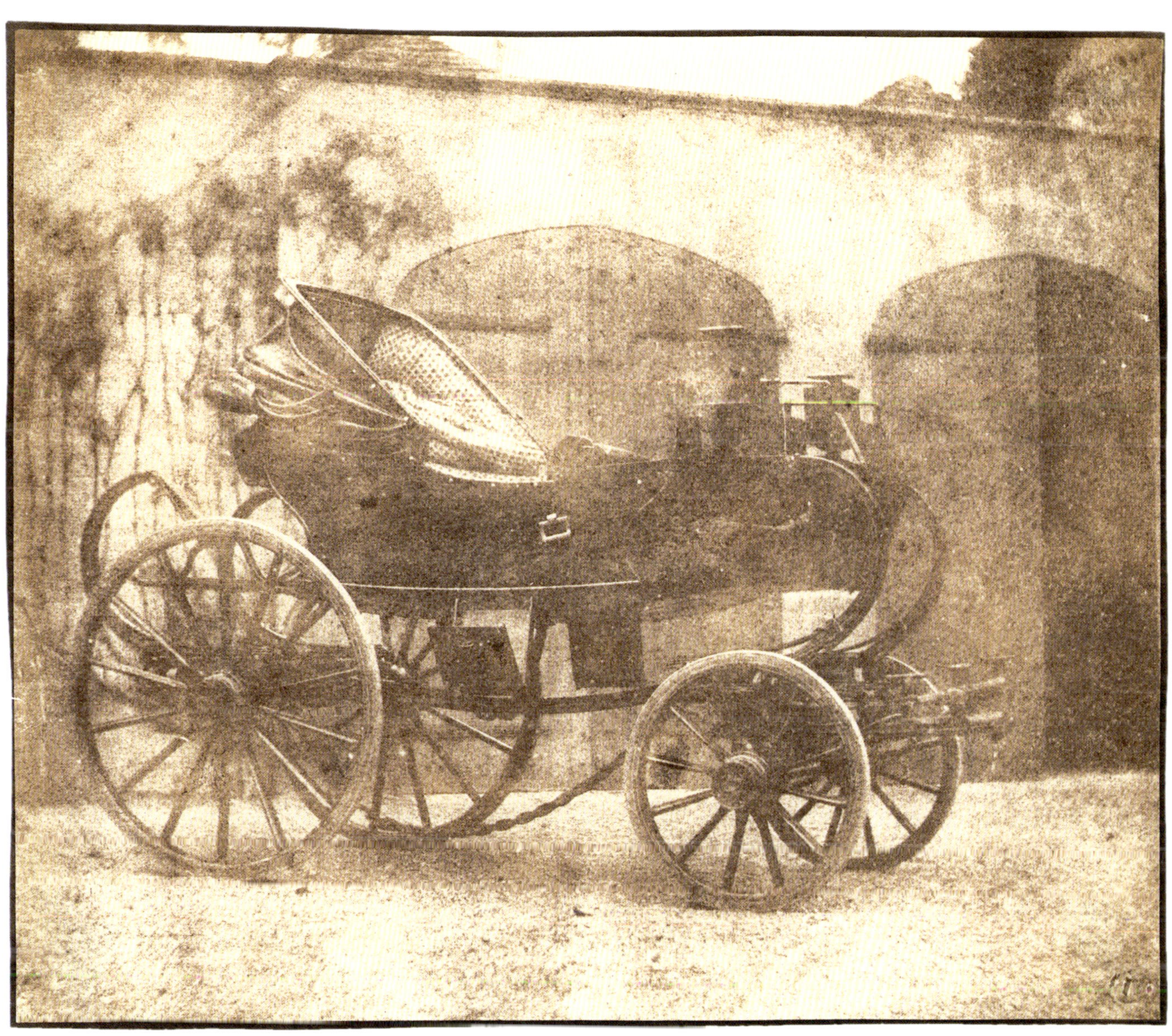

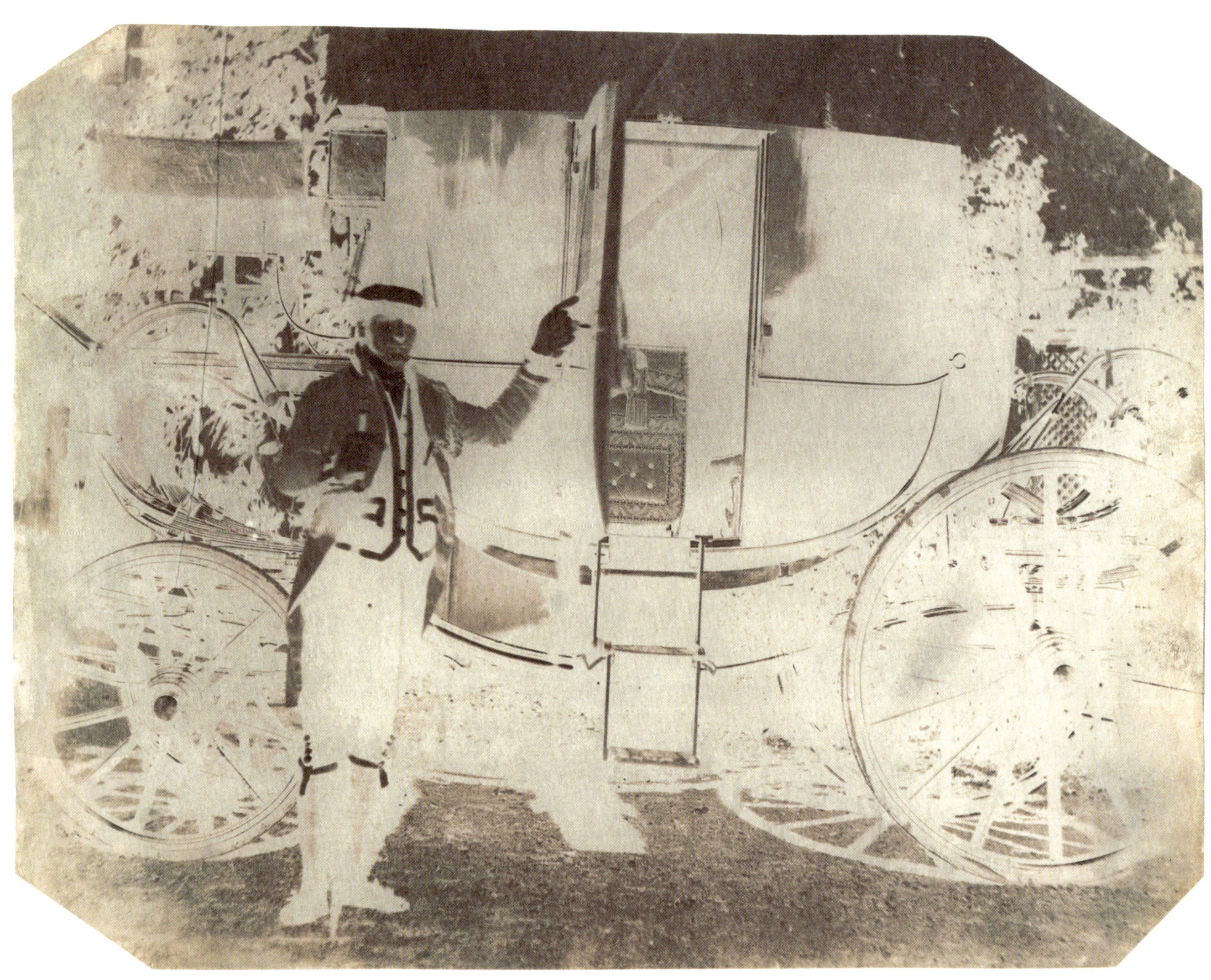

Footman at Carriage Door, October 14, 1840

Calotype negative, waxed, redeveloped by Harold White

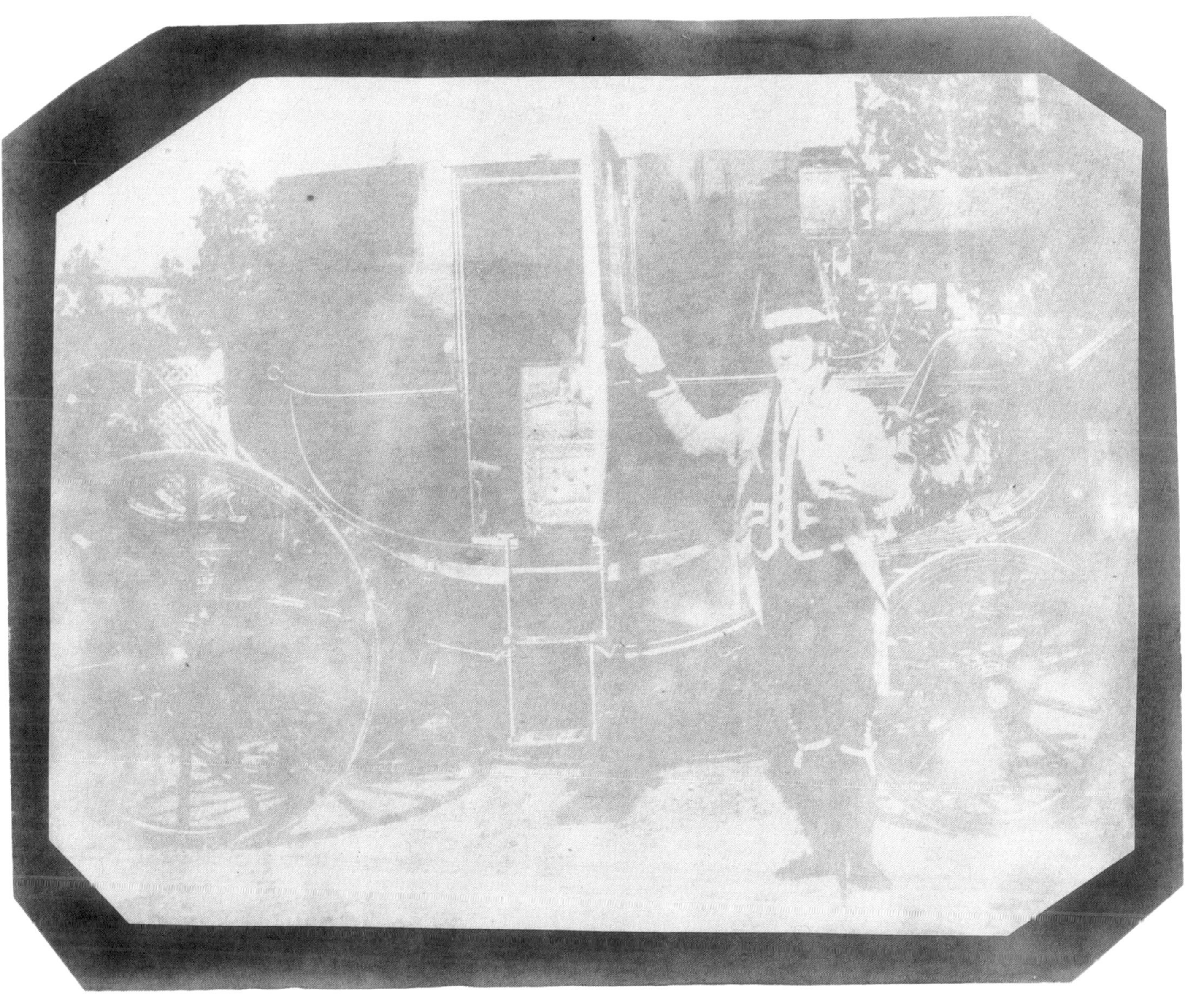

Footman at Carriage Door, October 14, 1840

Salted paper print from a calotype negative

Rev. Calvert Richard Jones and/or William Henry Fox Talbot
The Fruit Sellers, before December 13, 1845

Salted paper print from a calotype negative

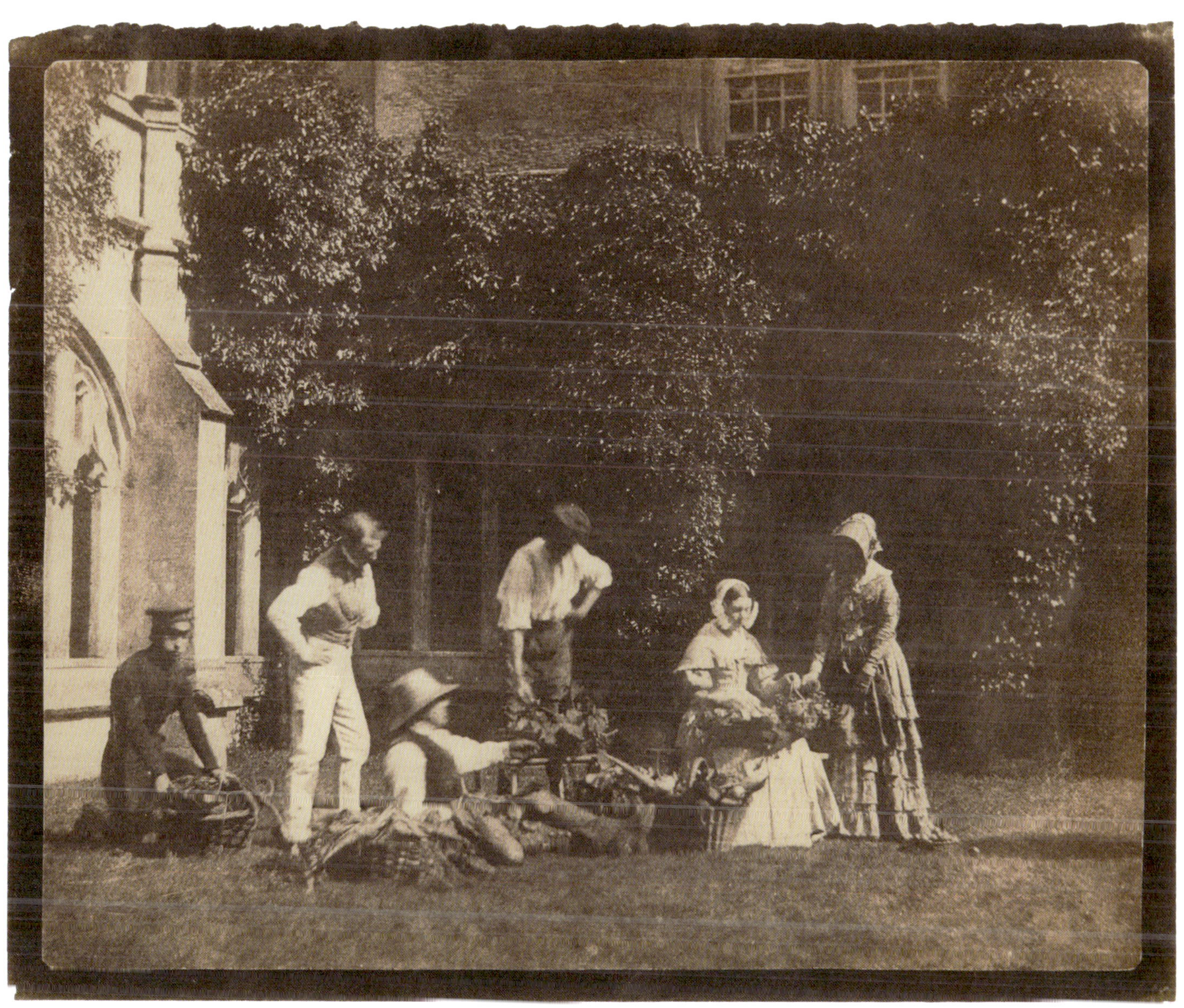

The Soliloquy of the Broom, January 21, 1841

Salted paper print from a calotype negative

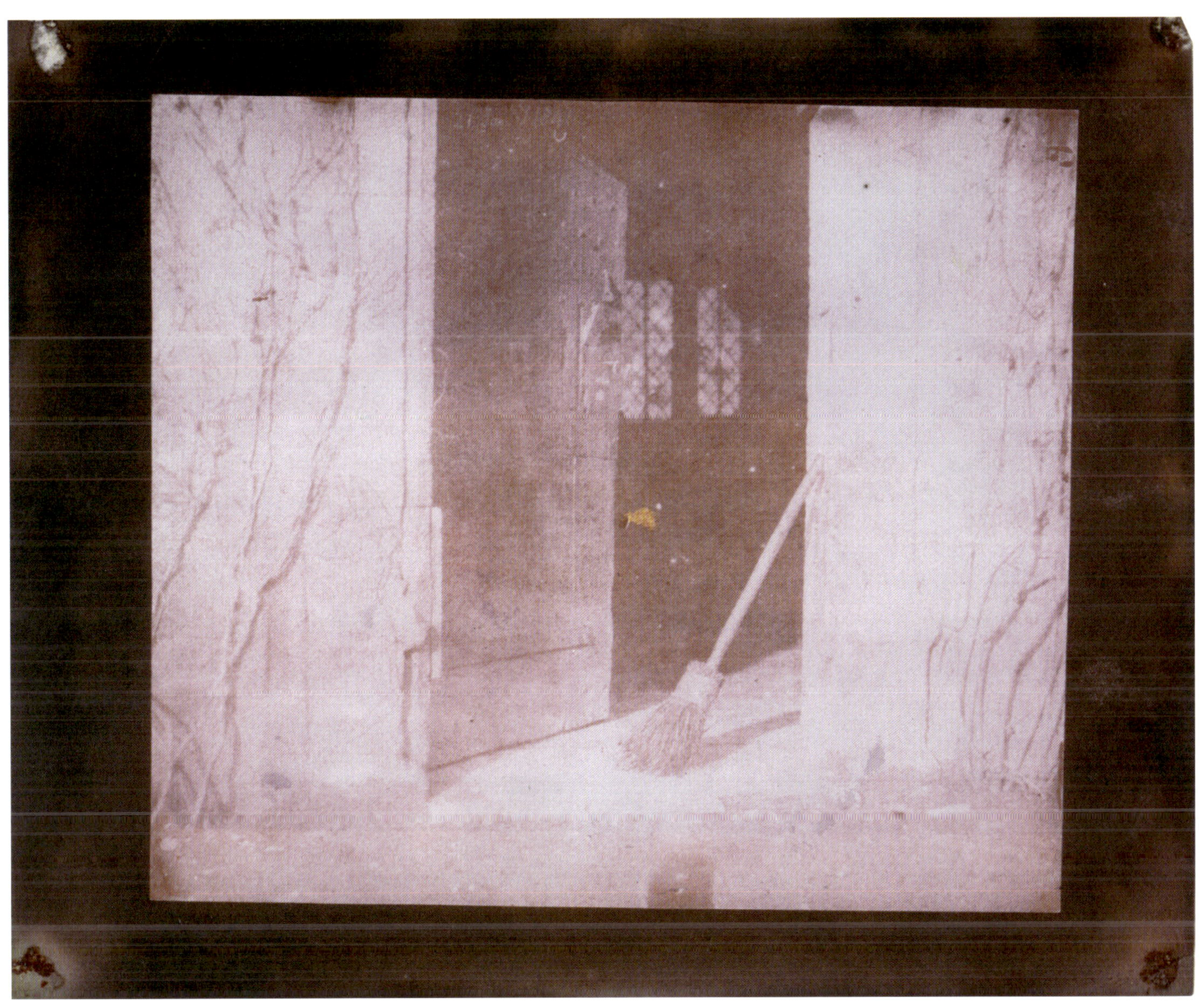

INTO THE WORLD

Talbot's first photogenic drawings of Oxford date to the summer of 1840, but most of his work there was with the calotype between 1841 and 1843. Although he was a Cambridge man, Oxford was far more convenient for transporting his equipment and chemicals from Lacock Abbey. Seduced by the university's ancient architecture, he wrote to his mother from there that "the weather has been exceedingly fine… and I have made about twenty views each day, some of which are very pretty — but the number of picturesque points of view seems almost inexhaustible"[1] He would use a later refinement of *Part of Queen's College, Oxford* as the first plate in *The Pencil of Nature*. Indeed, four of the twenty-four plates in the *Pencil* were taken in Oxford, including the magisterial *Gate below Tom Tower, Christ Church, Oxford*.

But Talbot's wanderlust continued to propel his photography. In 1841 he opined to his friend Sir John Herschel, "I must now really transport my apparatus to some locality where picturesque objects are to be met with, such as a Cathedral, or a seaport Town, for my own neighborhood is not particularly suited to the Artist, and offers no great variety of subjects."[2] As his Lacock photographs make clear, that assessment was a bit harsh, but the lure of the foreign was strong. In 1843 Talbot took his camera into the territory of his rival, Louis Jacques Mandé Daguerre, photographing at numerous places in France in preparation for *The Pencil of Nature*. Describing his effort to photograph *Le Château de Chambord*, he wrote, "I bent my footsteps towards this venerable pile. It was with the recollection of a long previous visit in May 1822. Chambord had ever dwelt upon my memory as one of the most remarkable objects I had seen in the course of my wanderings. Fortune did not altogether smile, for I was impeded by very unfavourable circumstances."[3] In spite of the miserable weather, Talbot captured not only the Château's elaborate elegance but also the debris that testified to the prolonged restoration of this stately "pile."

The city of Paris particularly stimulated Talbot's imagination and brought out a documentary side in him. He took dozens of images under the general title of "The Boulevards of Paris," recording scenes of life against the backdrop of elegant architecture. One of Talbot's most complex and telling photographs is his view of *Nelson's Column under Construction, Trafalgar Square*. His choice of a framing that truncated the tower in order to emphasize the public space reflected his sensitivity to the 1840s social disruptions in Europe. There was great trepidation about creating urban spaces large enough to hold mass protests, including Trafalgar Square, still a site of frequent demonstrations. Talbot understood both sides of this well, having skillfully guided the village of Lacock through the agricultural riots of the 1830s and subsequently becoming a Member of the First Reform Parliament in 1832. —LJS

1   Talbot to Elisabeth Feilding, September 6, 1843; transcribed in *The Correspondence of William Henry Fox Talbot*, Doc. No. 4875.

2   Talbot to Sir John Herschel, March 18, 1841, Royal Society, London; transcribed in *Correspondence*, Doc. No. 4218.

3   Expanded from Talbot's draft text for a plate in *The Pencil of Nature*; private collection.

Part of Queen's College, Oxford, early 1840s

Calotype negative, waxed

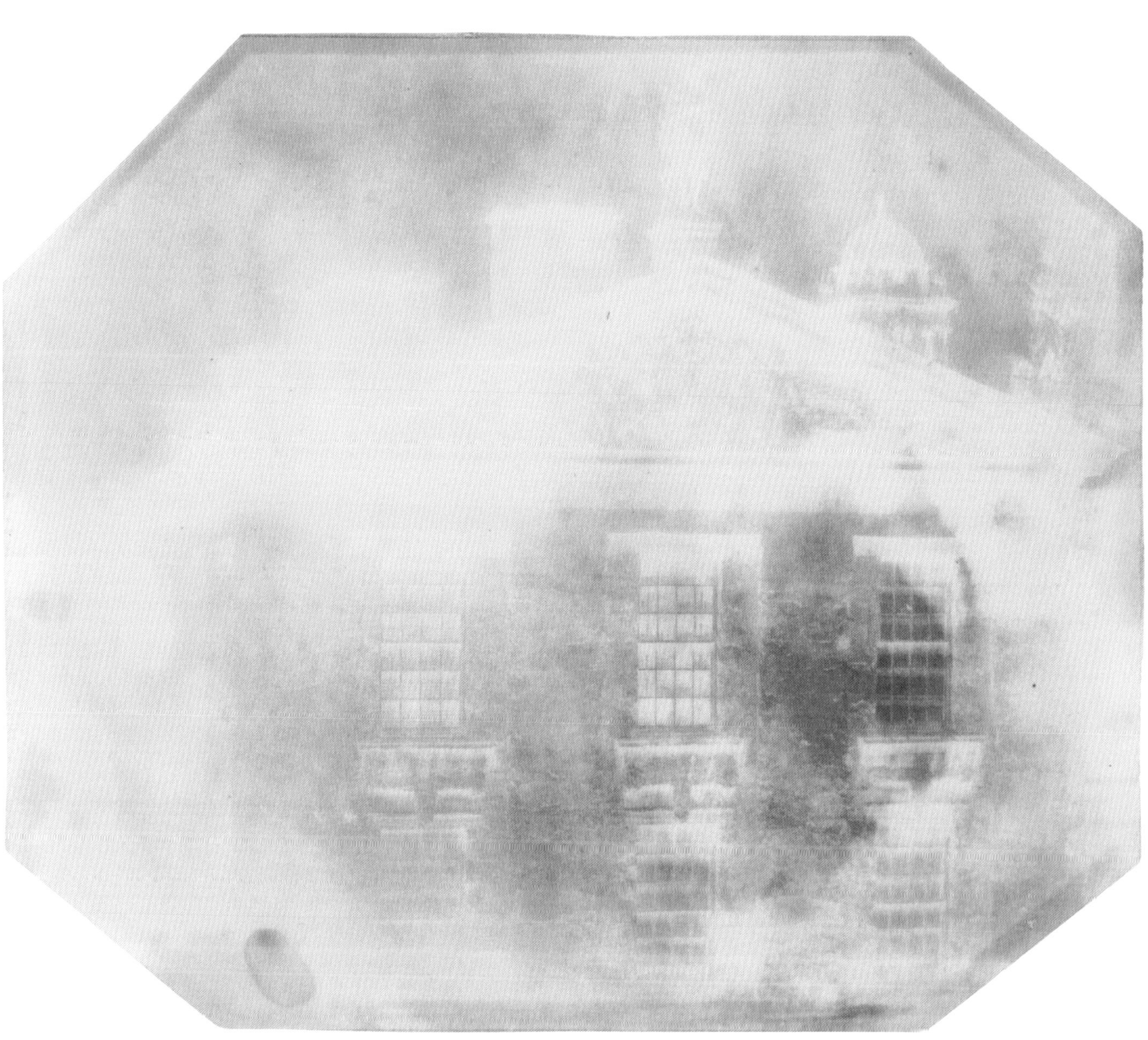

Rev. Calvert Richard Jones or William Henry Fox Talbot
Scene from a Window on rue de la Paix, Paris, ca. 1843–44

Calotype negative, waxed

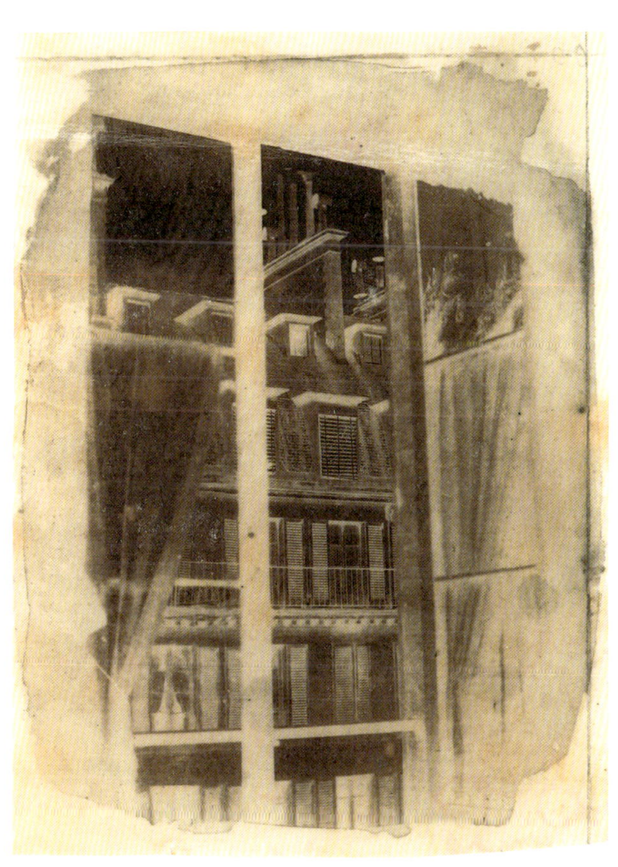

Townhouse on a Paris Boulevard, May/June 1843

Salted paper print from a calotype negative

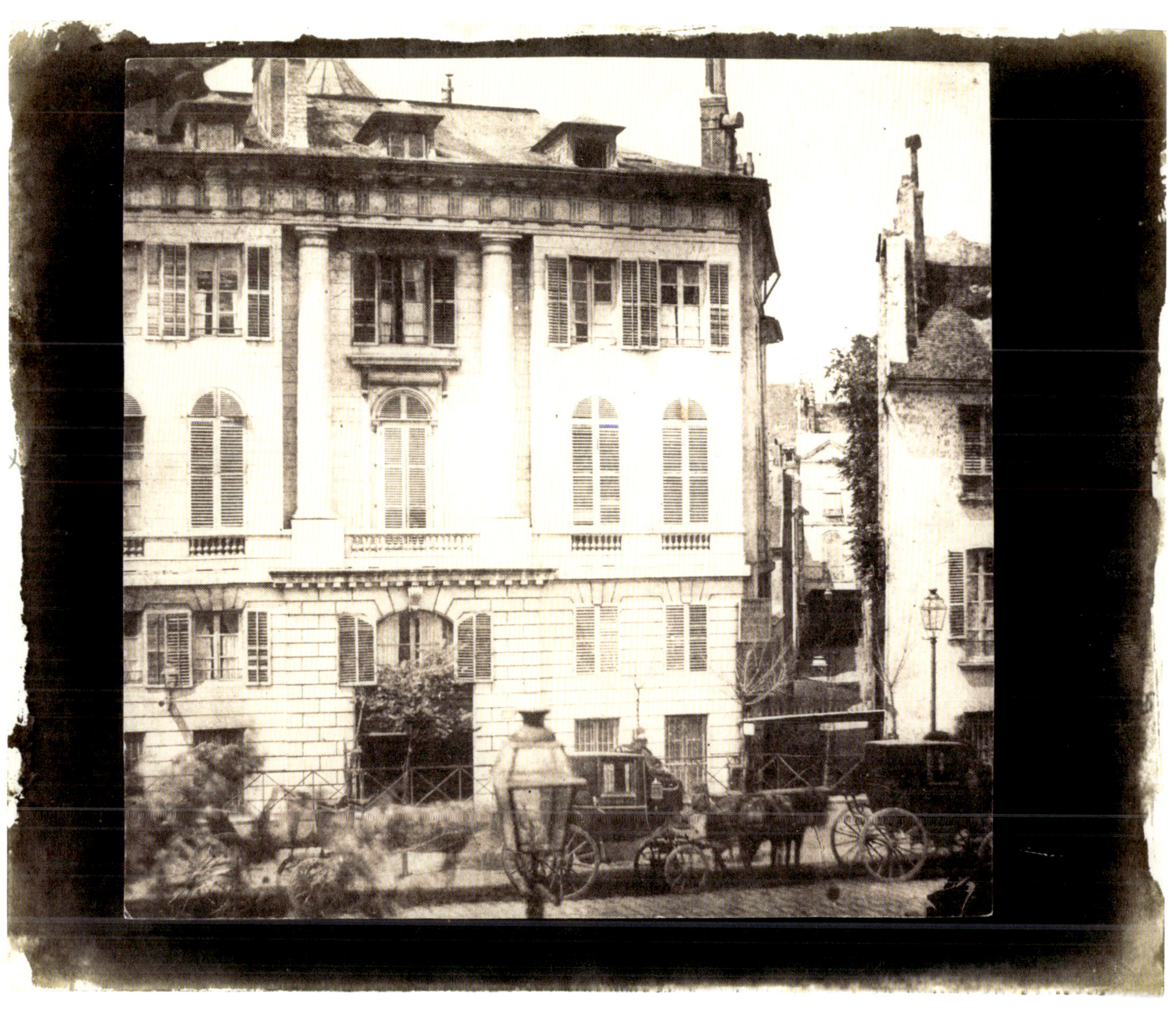

Le Château de Chambord, June 16, 1843

Salted paper print from a calotype negative

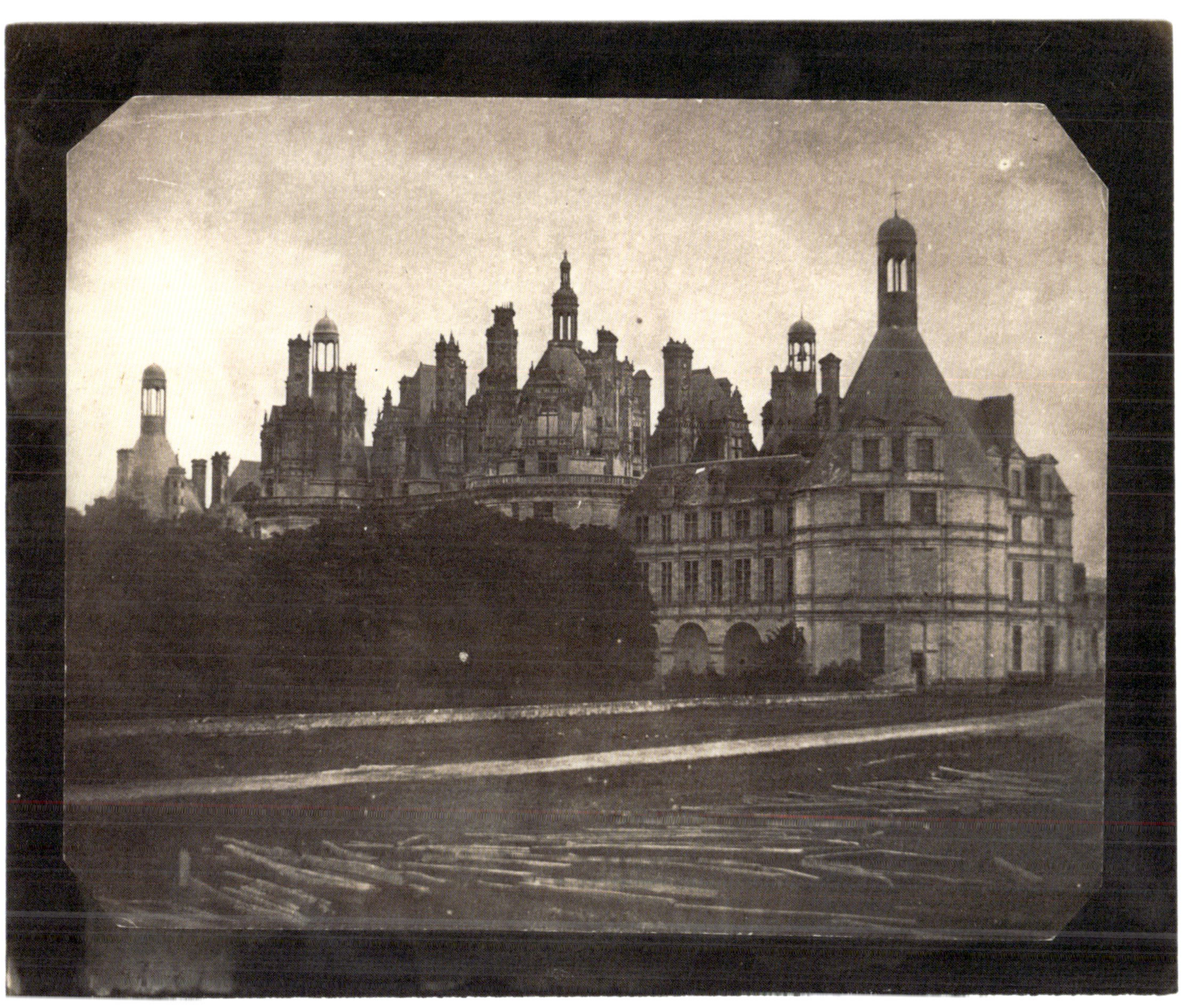

Gate below Tom Tower, Christ Church,
Oxford, prior to September 1844

Salted paper print from a calotype negative

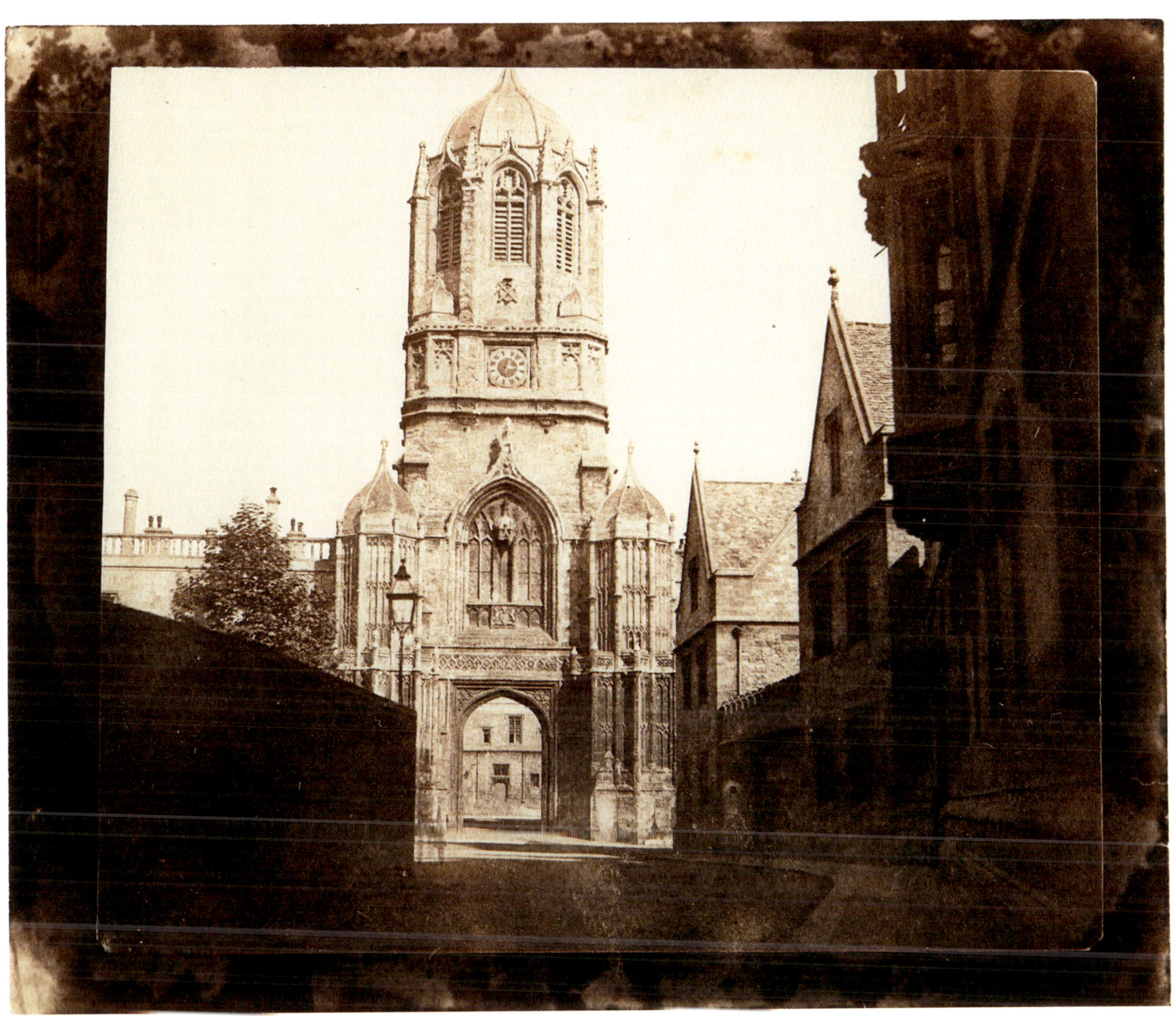

Nelson's Column under Construction, Trafalgar Square, first week of April 1844

Salted paper print from a calotype negative

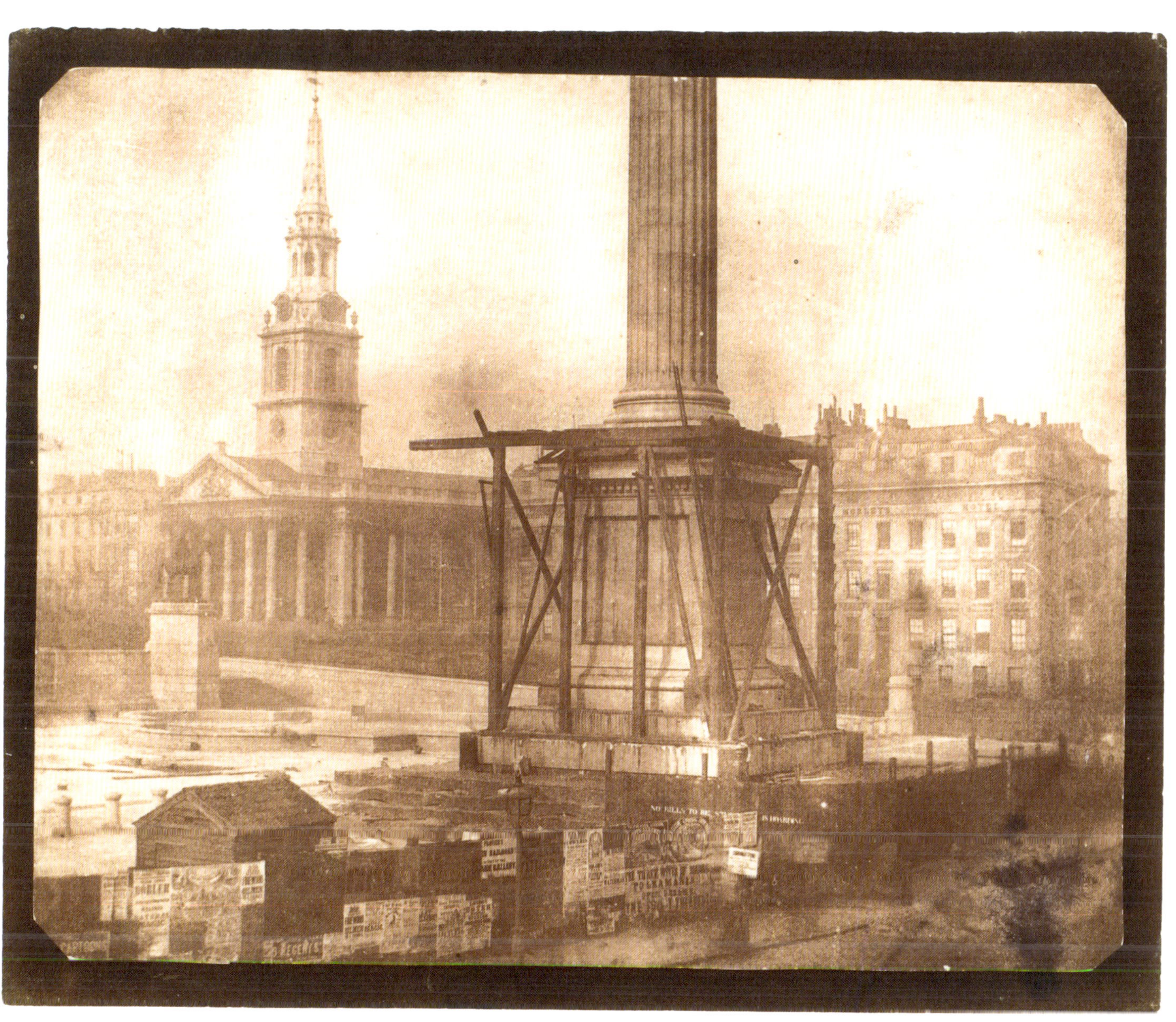
NO BILLS TO BE STUCK ON THIS HOARDING

The **TRANSIENCE** of
LIGHT

One of the most prescient observations about early photography was made by a reviewer of Talbot's *The Pencil of Nature* who marveled at how the new art "has already enabled us to hand down to future ages a picture of the sunshine of yesterday, or a memorial of the haze of to-day."[1] The sunshine of yesterday! Photography and time have always been intertwined in a complex way. As we have seen in Talbot's portraits of his daughters or in *Le Château de Chambord*, a photograph captures a very specific moment — a period in a child's growth or a particular stage of a building's reconstruction, for example. Yet once these transient moments were recorded on Talbot's magical paper, it was as if they were trapped in amber and preserved forever. Similarly, Talbot was able to arrest the immediate and fleeting experience of the magnified projections of a solar microscope. A period of bright sunshine would illuminate the tiny subject sufficiently for the photographic paper to trap it. That negative would then yield prints whose fine detail could be studied repeatedly in the parlor at will. This type of subject represented what Talbot saw as one of the greatest potentials for photography, the sharing of scientific and other information through accurate illustrations delivered economically to the masses.

Sculpture and photography have a natural affinity, for unlike the sharp lines of engravings, photography can record the subtleties of tone created by the sculpted surface modulating the light. Talbot found that photographing plaster busts allowed for an almost inexhaustible variety of effects: each angle, each direction and quality of light, and each cropping could represent the sculpture in a very specific way. Everyday objects, too, could be exploited for such effects. To take advantage of bright daylight, Talbot wheeled out into the Cloisters of Lacock Abbey a specially constructed set of shelves that became a stage where he could choreograph light itself. At times they were filled with articles of china and glass, which, though superficially similar in size and shape, each treated light very differently. Light wrapped around and only partially penetrated the Dresden porcelain, retaining its solid shapes, whereas with glass, light both refracted through and reflected off it. Was Talbot aware that he was taking a multiplicity of self-portraits in the reflections of the cut-glass objects? With present technology we cannot quite make these out, but they are there and perhaps someday there will be a way to tease them out.

Returning to one of Talbot's earliest calotypes, the *Oriel Windows*, we are again reminded of how much there is yet to understand in his work. He had a reverence for Nature's hand and would never retouch his negatives, and yet something motivated him in this case to trim his precious paper negative to its wild and seemingly arbitrary shape. It makes our eyes dance and perhaps just that was his intent. —LJS

1   *Athenæum*, no. 904 (February 22, 1845): 202.

Bust of Venus on a Round Tabletop, early 1840s

Salted paper print from a calotype negative

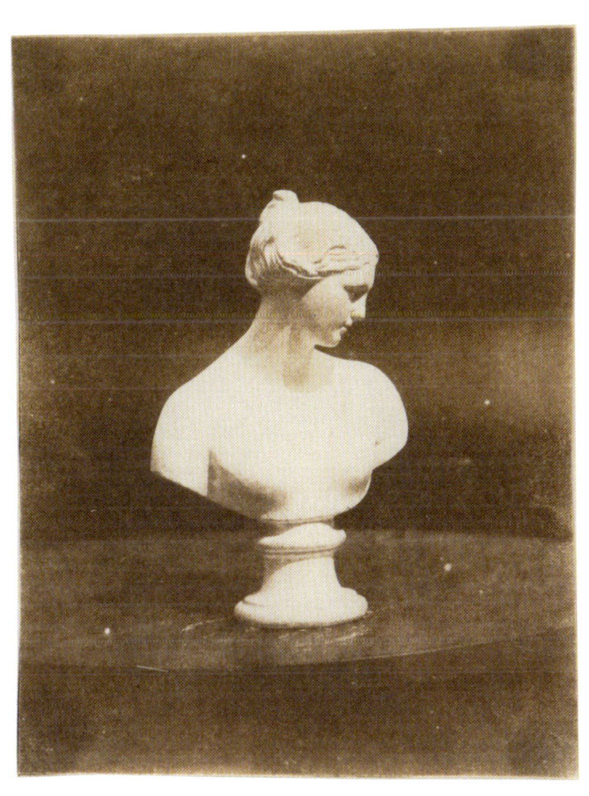

Bust of Patroclus, August 9, 1842

Salted paper print from a calotype negative

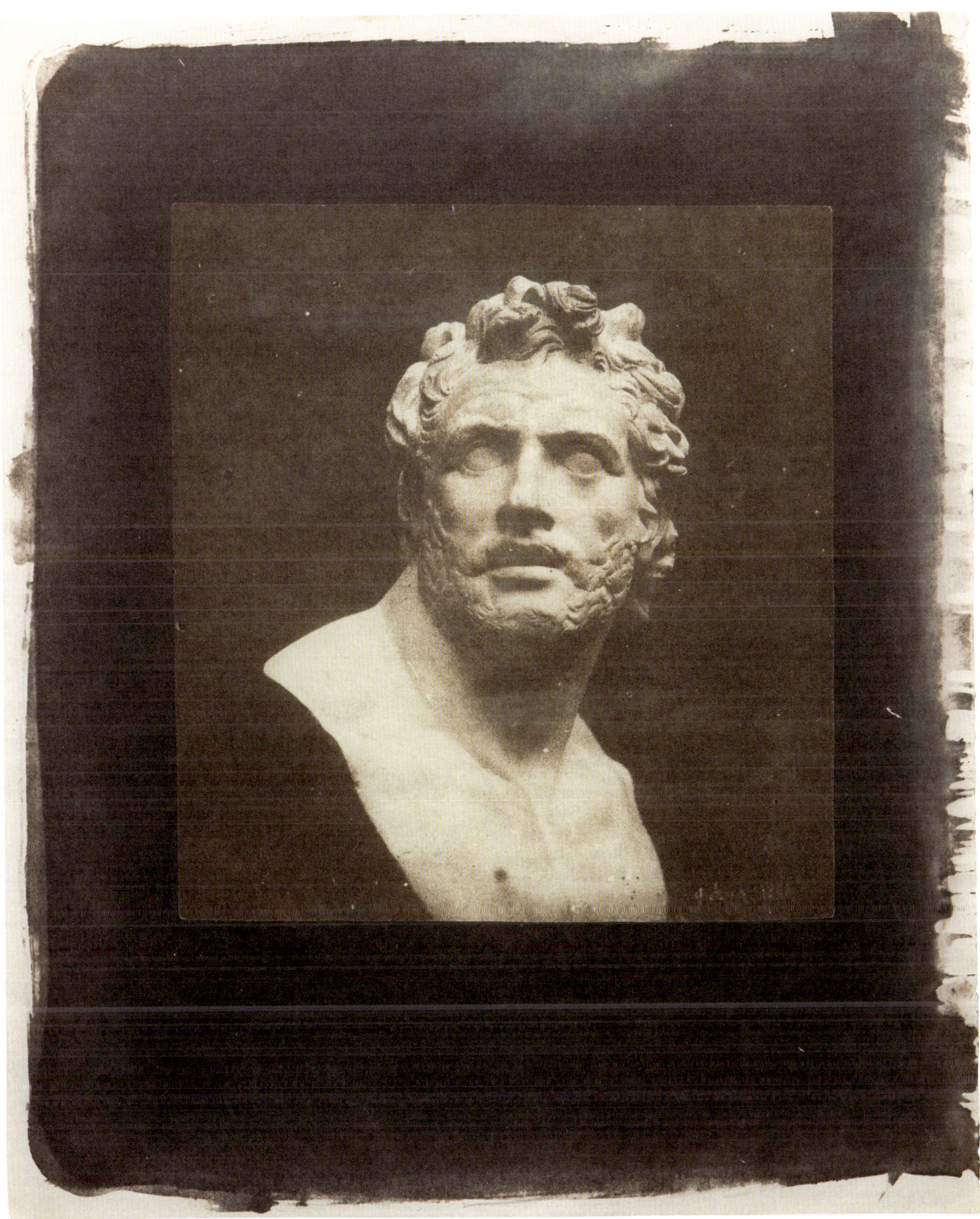

Slice of Horse Chestnut, in the Solar Microscope, May 28, 1840

Salted paper print from a photogenic drawing negative

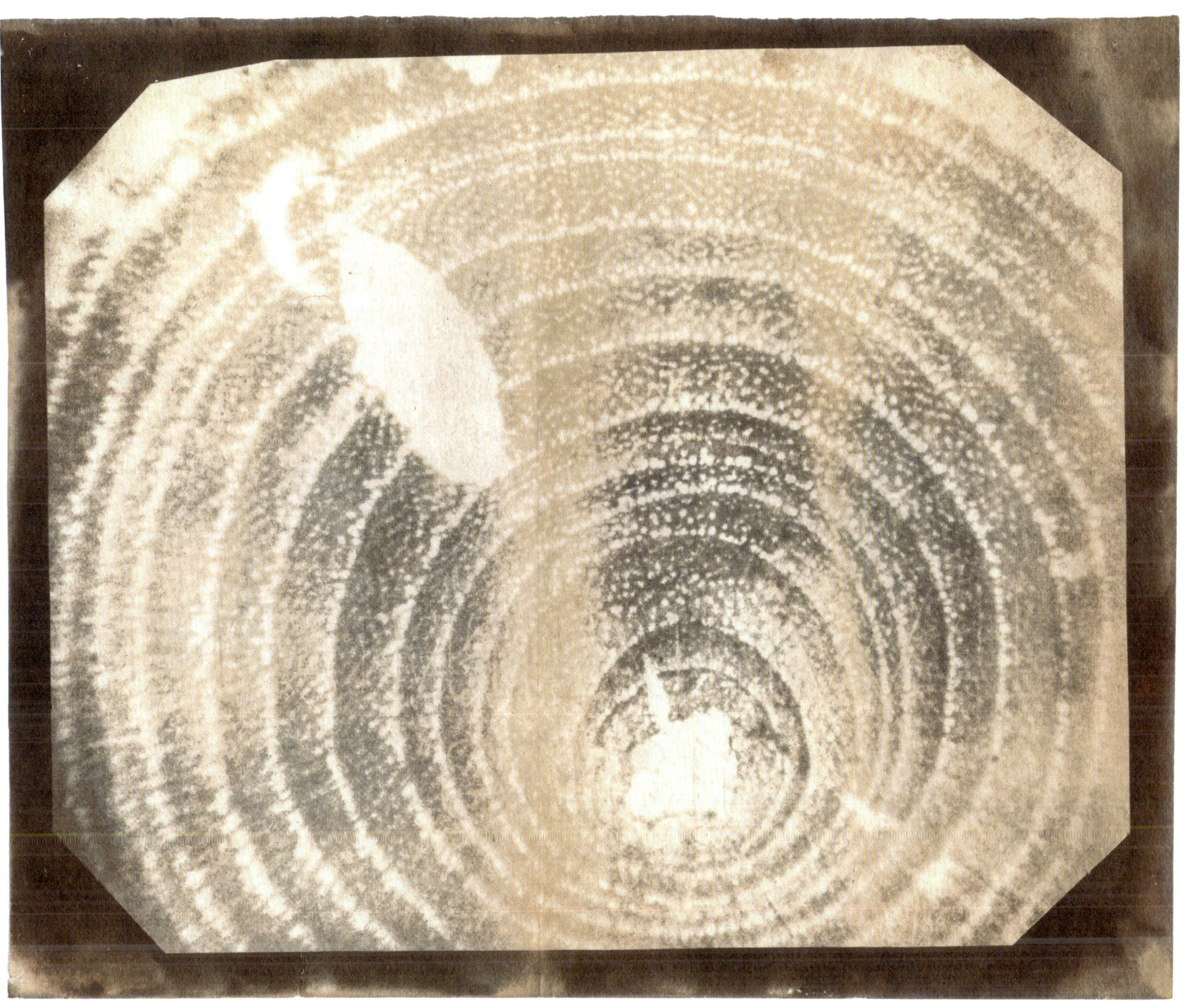

Articles of China, 1844

Salted paper print from a calotype negative

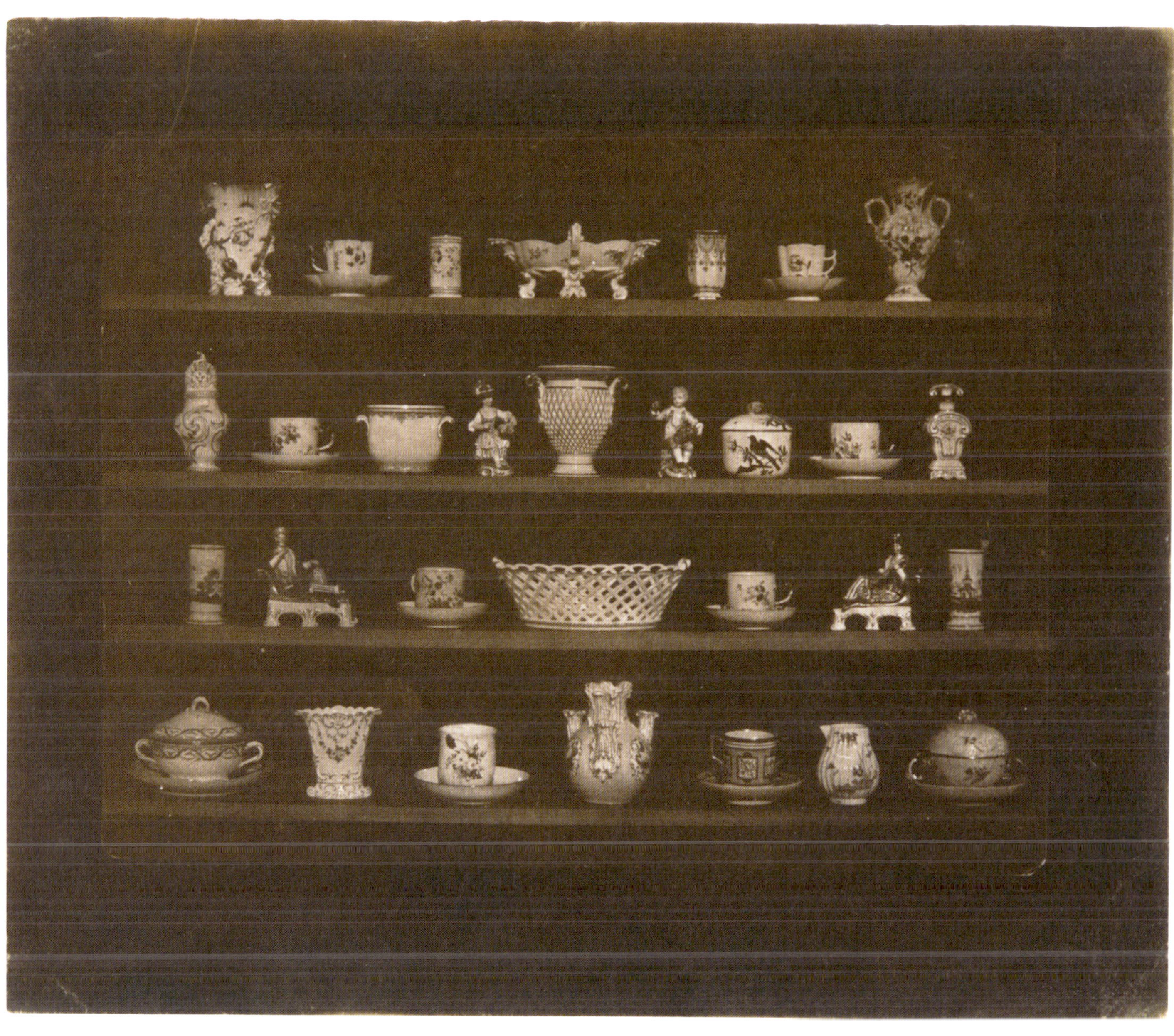

Articles of Glass, before June 1844

Salted paper print from a calotype negative

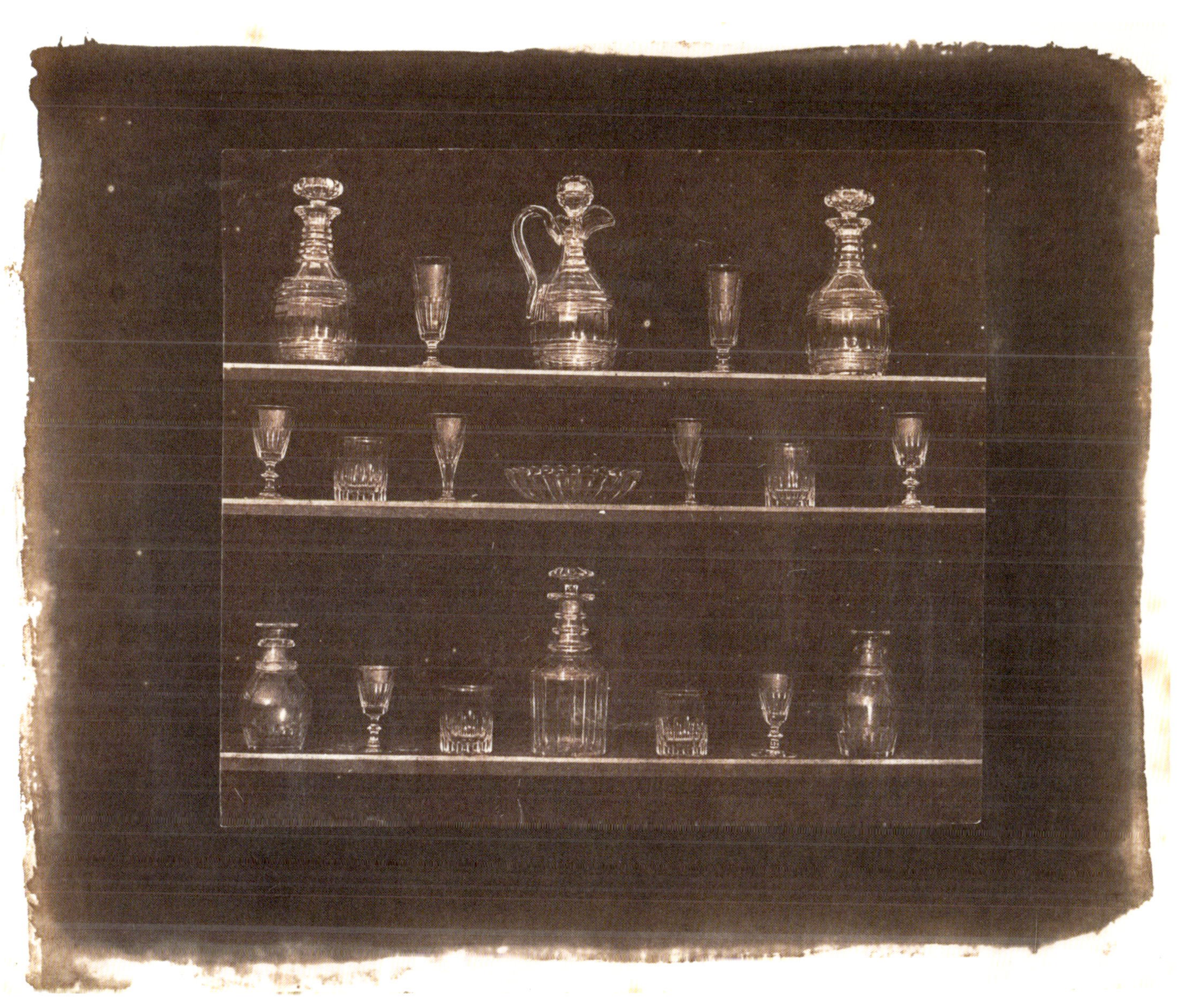

Oriel Windows, South Front of
Lacock Abbey, December 24, 1840

Salted paper print from a calotype negative

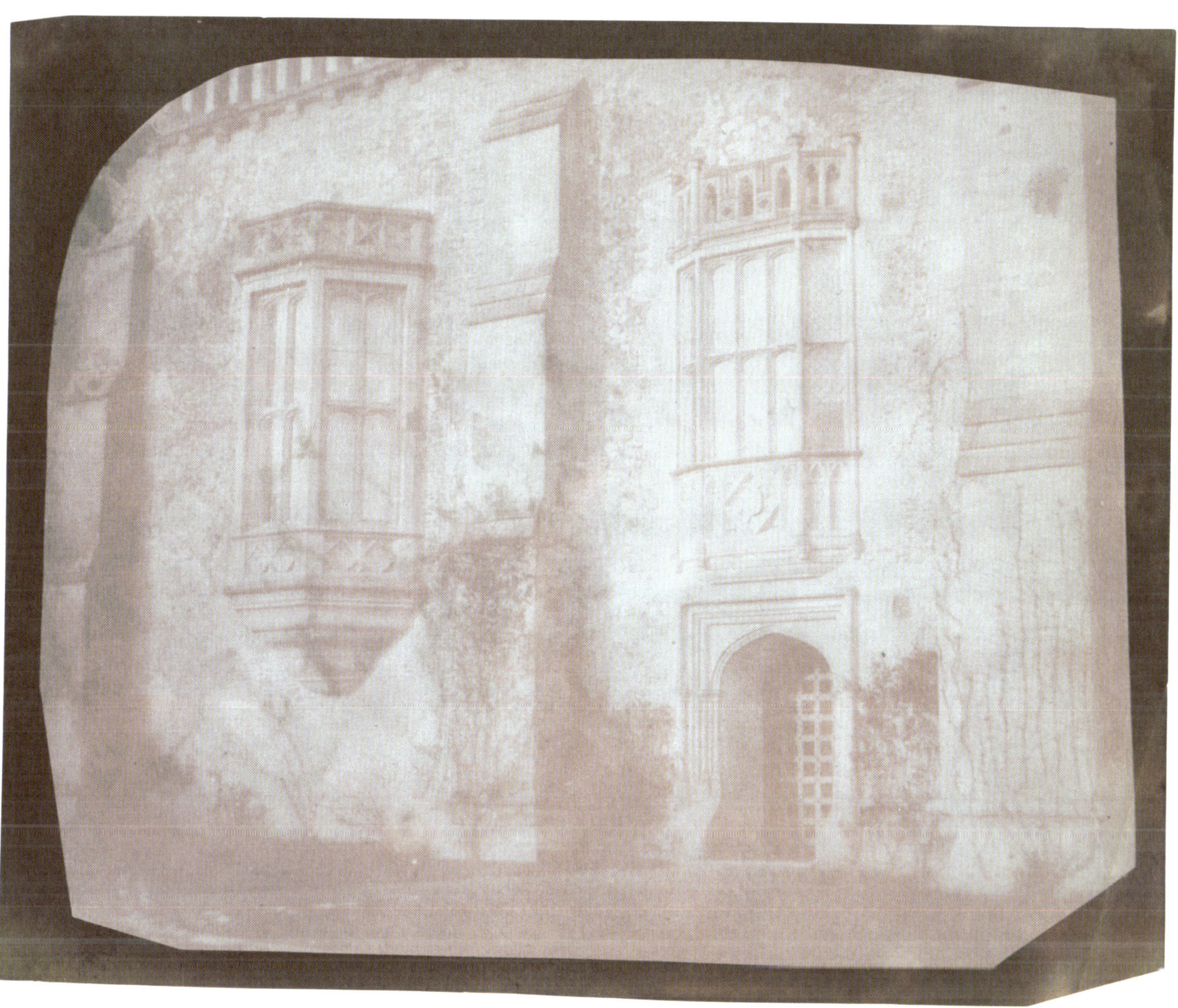

CHRONOLOGY

DAN LEERS

1800

FEBRUARY 11: William Henry Fox Talbot born at Melbury House in Dorset, England

JULY 30: William Davenport Talbot, Henry Fox Talbot's father, dies

1802

JUNE 22: Thomas Wedgwood and Humphry Davy publish their experiments in attempting to capture a photographic image

1804

APRIL 24: Lady Elisabeth Fox-Strangways, Talbot's mother, remarries Captain Charles Feilding

1808

SPRING: Talbot enters the school in Rottingdean, Sussex

1811

JULY: Enrolls at the Harrow School, London, and enters Dr. George Butler's House

1816

EARLY: Takes his first trip to the European continent

1817

JANUARY: Studies with Rev. Thomas Kaye Bonney at Normanton, Lincolnshire

LATE: Enters Trinity College, Cambridge, where he studies mathematics and classics

1820

Wins Porson University Prize in Greek verse

1821

FEBRUARY 11: Turns twenty-one and assumes all "investments, consoles and annuities," including the annual net income of approximately $200,000 (in 2017 dollars) generated by the estate

MARCH: Wins Chancellor's Classical Medal

Graduates from Cambridge University

1822

DECEMBER 13: Becomes a Fellow of the Astronomical Society

1824

SEPTEMBER 17 OR 18: Meets John Herschel in Munich

1825

Works for several weeks at the Paris Observatory with François Arago and Alexander von Humboldt

1826

JUNE: Publishes first paper on optics and light, titled "Some Experiments on Coloured Flames"

1827

Nicéphore Niépce successfully records part of his house on a pewter plate sensitized with bitumen to obtain what is now the oldest surviving photograph known

SUMMER: Talbot takes up residence in his familial home of Lacock Abbey, Wiltshire

1830

Publishes first novel, *Legendary Tales in Verse and Prose*, as well as a political pamphlet entitled "Thoughts on Moderate Reform in the House of Commons"

1831

Alters the South Gallery of Lacock Abbey to feature three oriel windows (see page 85)

MARCH 17: Becomes a Fellow of the Royal Society, London

APRIL 30: Loses first bid for parliamentary seat with a reform campaign

1832

DECEMBER 10: Wins election to Parliament

DECEMBER 20: Marries Constance Mundy at All Souls Cathedral, London

1833

OCTOBER: Strikes upon the idea of photography while on a trip to Italy with Constance

1834

FALL: Stays with family near Geneva, Switzerland, and experiments with the *cliché-verre* process

1835

ON OR SHORTLY AFTER FEBRUARY 28: Makes references to "photogenic" and "sciagraphic" processes, precursors to positives and negatives in photography

APRIL 25: Ela Theresa Talbot, Talbot's first child, is born

AUGUST: Talbot makes an image of the oriel windows at Lacock Abbey, which is now the oldest surviving negative known

1836–37

Elected a Royal Society Council Member

1837

MARCH 16: Rosamond Constance Talbot, Talbot's second child, is born

SEPTEMBER 2: Captain Charles Feilding dies

1838

Talbot receives a Royal Medal from the Royal Society for his research on integral calculus

1839

JANUARY 7: François Arago announces the invention of the daguerreotype process by Louis Jacques Mandé Daguerre in Paris

JANUARY 25: Michael Faraday announces Talbot's photogenic drawing process and displays a number of his photogenic drawings at the Royal Institution, London

JANUARY 31: Talbot reads his paper "Some Account of the Art of Photogenic Drawing" outlining the discovery of paper-based photography to the Royal Society

FEBRUARY 21: "Account of the Processes Employed in Photogenic Drawing" is read at the meeting of the Royal Society, in which Talbot describes the specifics of his process for others to try

FEBRUARY 25: Matilda "Tilly" Caroline Talbot, Talbot's third child, is born

FEBRUARY 25: First public use of the term "photographic" to describe Talbot's images

APRIL: Talbot makes his first positive print from a camera negative, showing the inside of a window in the South Gallery of Lacock Abbey

1840

FEBRUARY: Sir John Herschel first uses the terms "positive" and "negative" to describe photography

SEPTEMBER 17: Talbot discovers a new form of photography, which he calls the "leucotype" or "positive photogenic drawing"

SEPTEMBER 21: Discovers that gallic acid will develop a latent photographic image

DECEMBER: Makes paired photogenic drawings that are now the earliest known stereoscopic photographs

1841

FEBRUARY 8: Patents the "calotype" process

1842

FEBRUARY 2: Charles Henry Talbot, Talbot's fourth child, is born

Receives the Rumford Medal from the Royal Society for "many important discoveries made in photography"

1843

JUNE 1: Enters second photographic patent for "photography," which specifically covers the printing of photographs in books

1843–44

LATE 1843–EARLY 1844: Founds the Reading Establishment with photographer (and former valet) Nicolaas Henneman

1844–46

In six fascicles, publishes *The Pencil of Nature*, the first mass-produced book featuring photographic illustrations, with tipped-in photographs printed at the Reading Establishment

1845

Publishes *Sun Pictures in Scotland* with prints from the Reading Establishment

1846

MARCH 12: Lady Elisabeth Feilding dies

1851

JUNE 14: Participates in the first flash photography experiment at the Royal Institution, London

1852

OCTOBER 29: Patents the "photographic engraving" process

1858

APRIL 21: Patents the "photoglyphic engraving" process

1866–77

Focuses on Assyriology and publishes forty-eight papers during this period

1877

SEPTEMBER 17: William Henry Fox Talbot dies in his sleep at Lacock Abbey at the age of seventy-seven

SELECTED BIBLIOGRAPHY

HANNAH TURPIN

WORKS ADDRESSING WILLIAM HENRY FOX TALBOT'S CONTEMPORARY MOMENT

Arnold, H. J. P. *William Henry Fox Talbot: Pioneer of Photography and Man of Science*. London: Hutchinson Benham, 1977.

Booth, Arthur H. *William Henry Fox Talbot: Father of Photography*. London: A. Barker, 1965.

Brusius, Mirjam, Katrina Dean, and Chitra Ramalingam, eds. *William Henry Fox Talbot: Beyond Photography*. New Haven: Yale Center for British Art, Paul Mellon Centre for Studies in British Art, 2013.

Buckland, Gail. *Reality Recorded: Early Documentary Photography*. Greenwich, CT: New York Graphic Society, 1974.

Maimon, Vered. *Singular Images, Failed Copies: William Henry Fox Talbot and the Early Photograph*. Minneapolis: University of Minnesota Press, 2015.

Schaaf, Larry J. *Out of the Shadows: Herschel, Talbot, and the Invention of Photography*. New Haven: Yale University Press, 1992.

Taylor, Roger. *Impressed by Light: British Photographs from Paper Negatives, 1840–1860*. New York: Metropolitan Museum of Art; Washington, DC: National Gallery of Art; New Haven: Yale University Press, 2007.

Thomas, D. B. *The First Negatives: An Account of the Discovery and Early Use of the Negative-Positive Process*. London: Science Museum, 1964.

Ward, John, and Sara Stevenson. *Printed Light: The Scientific Art of William Henry Fox Talbot and David Octavius Hill with Robert Adamson*. Edinburgh: Scottish National Portrait Gallery, 1986.

Watson, Roger, and Helen Rappaport. *Capturing the Light: The Birth of Photography, a True Story of Genius and Rivalry*. New York: St. Martin's Griffin, 2015.

WORKS ADDRESSING WILLIAM HENRY FOX TALBOT'S PHOTOGRAPHY

Batchen, Geoffrey. *William Henry Fox Talbot*. London: Phaidon Press, 2008.

Buckland, Gail. *Fox Talbot and the Invention of Photography*. Boston: David R. Godine, 1980.

Gray, Michael, Arthur Ollman, and Carol McCusker. *First Photographs: William Henry Fox Talbot and the Birth of Photography*. New York: Powerhouse Books, 2002.

Jammes, André. *William H. Fox Talbot, Inventor of the Negative-Positive Process*. Translated by Maureen Oberli-Turner. New York: Macmillan Publishing, 1973.

Lassam, Robert. *Fox Talbot, Photographer*. Tisbury, England: Compton Press, 1979.

Roberts, Russell, ed. *Huellas de luz: El arte y los experimentos de William Henry Fox Talbot* [Footprints of Light: The Art and Experiments of William Henry Fox Talbot]. Madrid: Aldeasa; Museo Nacional Centro de Arte Reina Sofía, 2001.

Roberts, Russell, Michael Gray, and Anthony Burnett-Brown. *Specimens and Marvels: William Henry Fox Talbot and the Invention of Photography*. New York: Aperture Foundation, 2000.

Roberts, Russell, and Greg Hobson. *William Henry Fox Talbot: Dawn of the Photograph*. London: Scala Arts & Heritage Publishers, 2016.

Schaaf, Larry J. *The Photographic Art of William Henry Fox Talbot*. Princeton, NJ: Princeton University Press, 2000.

———. *William Henry Fox Talbot: Photographs from The J. Paul Getty Museum*. Los Angeles: J. Paul Getty Museum, 2002.

OTHER WRITINGS AND
FURTHER RESOURCES

Bodleian Libraries at
University of Oxford. *The
William Henry Fox Talbot
Catalogue Raisonné*. http://
foxtalbot.bodleian.ox.ac.uk/.

De Montfort University,
Leicester. *The Correspondence
of William Henry Fox Talbot*.
http://foxtalbot.dmu.ac.uk/.

History of Photography 26,
no. 2 (2002). Issue dedicated
to William Henry Fox Talbot.

Schaaf, Larry J. *Records of
the Dawn of Photography:
Talbot's Notebooks P & Q*.
Cambridge, England:
Cambridge University Press in
cooperation with the National
Museum of Photography,
Film and Television, 1996.

Weaver, Mike, ed. *Henry Fox
Talbot: Selected Texts and
Bibliography*. Oxford: Clio
Press, 1992. Republication of
texts written by Talbot,
including *The Magic Mirror*;
*The Antiquity of the Book of
Genesis: Illustrated by Some
New Arguments*; *Early
Researches in Photography*;
*Photogenic Drawings Exhibited
in 1839*; *Two Letters on
Calotype Photogenic Drawing*;
and *The Pencil of Nature*.

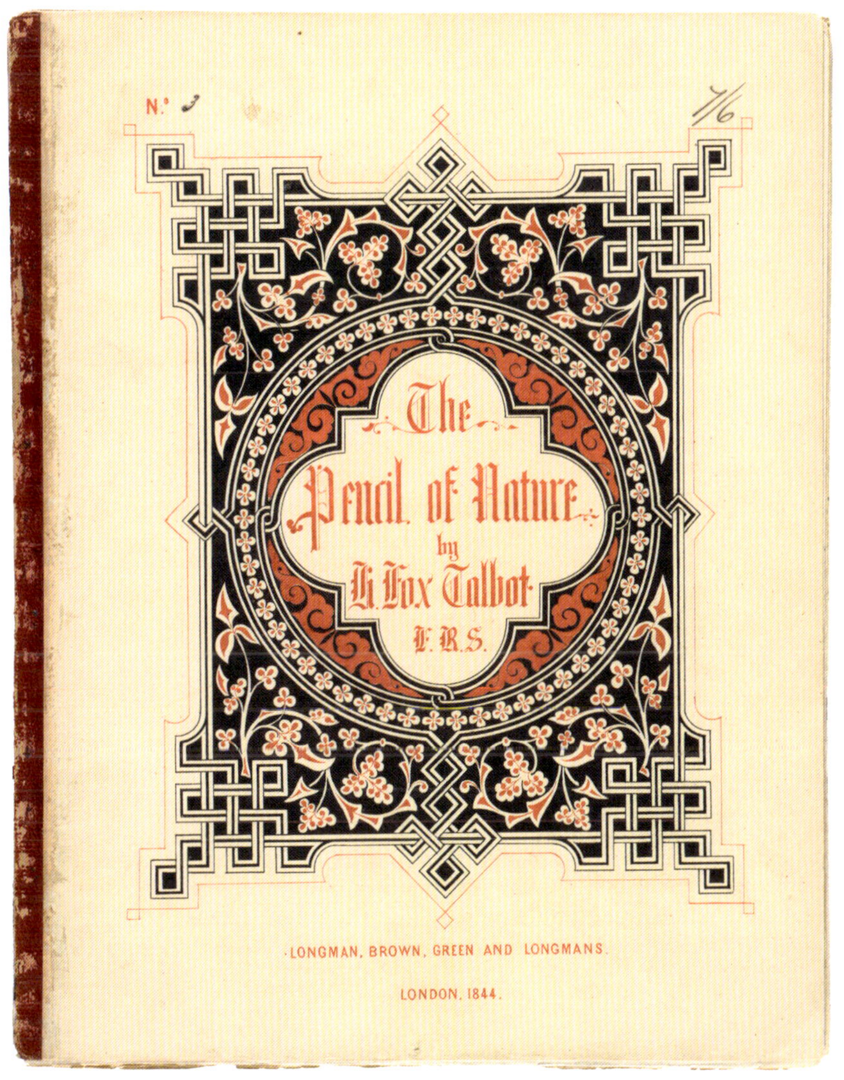

Cover of the third fascicle of
The Pencil of Nature (1845;
London: Longman, Brown, Green
and Longmans, 1844–46)
12 × 9½ in. (30.5 × 24.2 cm) closed
J. Paul Getty Museum, Los
Angeles, 84.XZ.571

CHECKLIST of the EXHIBITION

Unless otherwise noted, all works are by William Henry Fox Talbot (British, 1800–1877).

SC numbers correspond to the catalogue numbers in *The William Henry Fox Talbot Catalogue Raisonné* (http://foxtalbot .bodleian.ox.ac.uk/).

Buckler Fern, ca. 1839
Photogenic drawing negative
8⅝ × 7 in. (22 × 17.9 cm) (irregular)
Carnegie Museum of Art, Pittsburgh, Gift of William Talbott Hillman
SC 154
PAGE 25

Leaves and Flowers of a Plant, ca. 1839
Photogenic drawing negative
9 × 7³⁄₁₆ in. (22.8 × 18.2 cm) (corners trimmed)
Carnegie Museum of Art, Pittsburgh, Gift of William Talbott Hillman
SC 3736
PAGE 27

Trees in Winter, winter 1839–40
Salted paper print from a photogenic drawing negative
6 × 7½ in. (15.3 × 19.1 cm) image; 7 × 8⅝ in. (17.9 × 22 cm) sheet (corners trimmed)
Carnegie Museum of Art, Pittsburgh, Gift of William Talbott Hillman
SC 3828
PAGE 37

90

Lace, early 1840s
Salted paper print from a photogenic drawing negative
8¹⁵⁄₁₆ × 7⅜ in. (22.7 × 18.7 cm) image; 9 × 7⁷⁄₁₆ in. (22.9 × 18.8 cm) sheet
Carnegie Museum of Art, Pittsburgh, Purchased with funds provided by the William Talbott Hillman Foundation, 2017.2.1
SC 2818
PAGE 33

Bust of Venus on a Round Tabletop, early 1840s
Salted paper print from a calotype negative
3⅞ × 3 in. (9.9 × 7.5 cm)
Carnegie Museum of Art, Pittsburgh, Gift of William Talbott Hillman, 2017.30.1
SC 212
PAGE 75

Part of Queen's College, Oxford, early 1840s
Calotype negative, waxed
6¼ × 7³⁄₁₆ in. (15.8 × 18.2 cm) (corners trimmed)
The William Talbott Hillman Collection, Promised gift to Carnegie Museum of Art, Pittsburgh
SC 1584
PAGE 61

Slice of Horse Chestnut, in the Solar Microscope, May 28, 1840
Salted paper print from a photogenic drawing negative
6¹¹⁄₁₆ × 8⅛ in. (16.9 × 20.6 cm) image; 7⁵⁄₁₆ × 8¾ in. (18.6 × 22.3 cm) sheet
Hans P. Kraus Jr., New York
SC 2432
PAGE 79

Footman at Carriage Door, October 14, 1840
Calotype negative, waxed, redeveloped by Harold White
6⁷⁄₁₆ × 8¼ in. (16.3 × 21 cm) (corners trimmed)
Hans P. Kraus Jr., New York
SC 2507
PAGE 52

Footman at Carriage Door, October 14, 1840
Salted paper print from a calotype negative
6⁷⁄₁₆ × 8¼ in. (16.3 × 21 cm) image; 7³⁄₁₆ × 8¹⁵⁄₁₆ in. (18.3 × 22.7 cm) sheet (corners trimmed)
Private collection, courtesy of Hans P. Kraus Jr., New York
SC 2507
PAGE 53

Oriel Windows, South Front of Lacock Abbey, December 24, 1840
Salted paper print from a calotype negative
6¾ × 8⅜ in. (17.2 × 21.3 cm) image (irregular); 7⁵⁄₁₆ × 9 in. (18.6 × 22.8 cm) sheet
Hans P. Kraus Jr., New York
SC 2540
PAGE 85

The Soliloquy of the Broom, January 21, 1841
Salted paper print from a calotype negative
6 × 6⅞ in. (15.3 × 17.5 cm) image; 7⁷⁄₁₆ × 8⅞ in. (18.8 × 22.5 cm) sheet
Private collection, courtesy of Hans P. Kraus Jr., New York
SC 2548
PAGE 57

Wild Fennel, 1841–42
Salted paper print
7⅜ × 8¹⁵⁄₁₆ in. (18.7 × 22.7 cm) (corners trimmed)
The Metropolitan Museum of Art, New York, Gilman Collection, Purchase, Denise and Andrew Saul Gift, 2005, 2005.100.260
SC 757
PAGE 29

Scene in a Wood, summer 1842
Salted paper print from a calotype negative
6¼ × 7⅝ in. (15.8 × 19.4 cm) image; 7¹³⁄₁₆ × 9¹³⁄₁₆ in. (19.9 × 25 cm) sheet
Private collection, courtesy of Hans P. Kraus Jr., New York
SC 97
PAGE 39

Bust of Patroclus, August 9, 1842
Salted paper print from a calotype negative
5⅛ × 5 in. (13.8 × 12.9 cm) image; 9 × 7½ in. (23.1 × 19.1 cm) sheet
Carnegie Museum of Art, Pittsburgh, Gift of William Talbott Hillman, 2017.30.3
SC 190
PAGE 77

Oak Tree in Winter, 1842–43
Salted paper print from a calotype negative
7¹¹⁄₁₆ × 6⁹⁄₁₆ in. (19.5 × 16.6 cm) image; 9⅜ × 7¾ in. (23.8 × 19.7 cm) sheet
Carnegie Museum of Art, Pittsburgh, Gift of the William Talbott Hillman Foundation
SC 1981
PAGE 41

Townhouse on a Paris Boulevard, May/June 1843
Salted paper print from a calotype negative
6⅝ × 6¾ in. (16.8 × 17.1 cm) image; 7⅜ × 9 in. (18.7 × 22.8 cm) sheet
Collection of Michael Mattis and Judith Hochberg, New York
SC 129
PAGE 65

Le Château de Chambord, June 16, 1843
Salted paper print from a calotype negative
6⁵⁄₁₆ × 8¹⁄₁₆ in. (16 × 20.4 cm) image; 7⁷⁄₁₆ × 9¹⁄₁₆ in. (18.8 × 23 cm) sheet
Hans P. Kraus Jr., New York
SC 1164
PAGE 67

Rev. Calvert Richard Jones
(Welsh, 1802–1877) or William
Henry Fox Talbot
*Scene from a Window
on rue de la Paix, Paris*,
ca. 1843–44
Calotype negative, waxed
4⅜ × 3³⁄₁₆ in. (11.1 × 8.1 cm)
Hans P. Kraus Jr., New York
SC 2702
PAGE 63

*Nelson's Column under
Construction, Trafalgar
Square*, first week of April 1844
Salted paper print from a
calotype negative
6¾ × 8⅝ in. (17.1 × 21.2 cm) image;
7⅜ × 8⅞ in. (18.7 × 22.5 cm) sheet
The Metropolitan Museum of
Art, New York, Anonymous Gift
and Purchase, Alfred Stieglitz
Society Gifts; 2004 Benefit Fund;
W. Bruce and Delaney H. Lundberg
Gift; The Horace W. Goldsmith
Foundation Fund, through Joyce
and Robert Menschel; Susan
and Thomas Dunn and Constance
and Leonard Goodman Gifts,
2009, 2009.279
SC 3662
PAGE 71

*A Barouche in the North
Courtyard of Lacock Abbey*,
April 1844
Salted paper print from a
calotype negative
6 × 7 in. (15.2 × 17.9 cm) image;
6¹⁄₁₆ × 7³⁄₁₆ in. (15.5 × 18.2 cm) sheet
Carnegie Museum of Art,
Pittsburgh, Gift of William Talbott
Hillman, 2017.30.2
SC 2760
PAGE 51

*Matilda and Ela Talbot
in the Cloisters at Lacock
Abbey*, April 1844
Right half of a salted paper print
from a calotype negative
6 × 3⅝ in. (15.2 × 9.2 cm) image;
6³⁄₁₆ × 3¹¹⁄₁₆ in. (15.7 × 9.4 cm) sheet
(corners trimmed)
The William Talbott Hillman
Collection, Promised gift
to Carnegie Museum of Art,
Pittsburgh
SC 2773
PAGE 49

*Rosamond Talbot in the
Cloisters at Lacock Abbey*,
April 1844
Left half of a salted paper print
from a calotype negative
6 × 3¹³⁄₁₆ in. (15.3 × 9.8 cm) image;
6³⁄₁₆ × 3¹⁵⁄₁₆ in. (15.7 × 10 cm) sheet
(corners trimmed)
The William Talbott Hillman
Collection, Promised gift
to Carnegie Museum of Art,
Pittsburgh
SC 2773
PAGE 48

Articles of China, 1844
Salted paper print from a
calotype negative
5½ × 7³⁄₁₆ in. (14 × 18.2 cm) image;
7⅜ × 8¾ in. (18.7 × 22.2 cm) sheet
Carnegie Museum of Art,
Pittsburgh, Purchased with funds
provided by the William Talbott
Hillman Foundation, 2017.2.2
SC 66
PAGE 81

Articles of Glass, before
June 1844
Salted paper print from a
calotype negative
5³⁄₁₆ × 5¹⁵⁄₁₆ in. (13.2 × 15.1 cm) image;
7½ × 9⅛ in. (19 × 23.2 cm) sheet
The Metropolitan Museum of Art,
New York, Purchase, The Horace
W. Goldsmith Foundation
Gift through Joyce and Robert
Menschel and Harrison D. Horblit
Gift, 1988, 1988.1047
SC 69
PAGE 83

*Gate below Tom Tower,
Christ Church, Oxford*, prior to
September 1844
Salted paper print from a
calotype negative
6⅝ × 7¾ in. (16.8 × 19.7 cm) image;
7⁷⁄₁₆ × 8¹⁵⁄₁₆ in. (19 × 22.7 cm) sheet
Carnegie Museum of Art,
Pittsburgh, Gift of the William
Talbott Hillman Foundation
SC 913
PAGE 69

Loch Katrine, October 1844
Salted paper print from a
caloytpe negative
7 × 8½ in. (17.8 × 21.8 cm) image;
7½ × 8⅞ in. (18.9 × 22.5 cm) sheet
Hans P. Kraus Jr., New York
SC 2787
PAGE 45

*An Aged Red Cedar Tree
in the Grounds of Mount
Edgcumbe*, ca. 1845
Salted paper print, varnished, from
a calotype negative
6¼ × 7¾ in. (15.8 × 19.6 cm) image;
7¼ × 8¾ in. (18.4 × 22.1 cm) sheet
Collection of Michael Mattis
and Judith Hochberg, New York
SC 22
PAGE 43

*Nicolaas Henneman
Showing an Album to Charles
Porter*, ca. 1845
Salted paper print from a
calotype negative
5¹⁵⁄₁₆ × 7⅝ in. (15.1 × 19.3 cm) image;
6 × 7¹¹⁄₁₆ in. (15.3 × 19.6 cm) sheet
The Metropolitan Museum of Art,
New York, Bequest of Maurice B.
Sendak, 2012, 2013.159.63
SC 992
FRONTISPIECE

Rev. Calvert Richard Jones
(Welsh, 1802–1877) and/or
William Henry Fox Talbot
The Fruit Sellers, before
December 13, 1845
Salted paper print from a
calotype negative
6¹¹⁄₁₆ × 8¼ in. (16.9 × 21 cm) image;
7⅛ × 8¾ in. (18.1 × 22.2 cm) sheet
Carnegie Museum of Art,
Pittsburgh, Gift of the William
Talbott Hillman Foundation
SC 1917
PAGE 55

Nicolaas Henneman
(Dutch, 1813–1898)
Portrait of an Unknown Man,
ca. 1844
Calotype negative
4½ × 3¾ in. (11.6 × 9.9 cm)
Carnegie Museum of Art,
Pittsburgh, Gift of William Talbott
Hillman, 2017.30.4
SC 1546
PAGE 17

Attributed to Nicolaas Henneman
(Dutch, 1813–1898)
Black Cherry Leaves,
mid–1840s
Photogenic drawing negative
7¼ × 9 in. (18.5 × 22.6 cm)
The William Talbott Hillman
Collection, Promised gift
to Carnegie Museum of Art,
Pittsburgh
SC 4202
PAGE 31

ACKNOWLEDGMENTS

Traditionally, museums have been siloed institutions divided into departments by geography, time period, or artistic medium, with curators specializing in a single area. From its inception, photography did not fit this model because of its roots in so many different fields. One of the reasons for these connections is that photography's inventor, William Henry Fox Talbot, had wide-ranging interests in nearly every subject imaginable.

In my own curatorial work, I also seek to create connections across departments and eras. For this reason, I feel fortunate to have focused on photography. Its links to painting, drawing, sculpture, and film, not to mention its scientific and technical applications, make it the ultimate bridge. Working on this exhibition and book, I was inspired by Talbot's prescience in understanding photography's promise. Nearly from the beginning, he realized it could record more accurately than the human hand, it could be readily reproduced and disseminated, and it could preserve a fleeting moment in time indefinitely. These elements continue to be relevant today.

This project was sparked by the passion of our most ardent supporter and collector, William Talbott Hillman, who shares my love of Talbot's work. None of this would have been possible without Bill's exceptional generosity. His donations of work by Talbot to the museum and his Foundation's support for our programming have created an enduring legacy for this institution.

A debt of gratitude is also owed to Dave Roger, president of the Hillman Family Foundations. Dave has been a critical interlocutor between the museum and the Foundations. He understands the significance of this project to everyone involved and was one of its first advocates.

Lynn Zelevansky, Henry J. Heinz II Director, provided early and continued support and vision for both the exhibition and the catalogue. Thanks are also due to Catherine Evans, chief curator, for her knowledge of the field and her nurturing presence. We are deeply indebted to Larry J. Schaaf, who, in addition to contributing insightful texts to the catalogue, freely shared his boundless knowledge of all things Talbot.

We are grateful to the lenders to this exhibition, especially Hans P. Kraus Jr. and Shelley Dowell at Hans P. Kraus Jr., Inc. They connected us to several private collectors who generously lent works to the show. At the Metropolitan Museum of Art, Jeff Rosenheim, curator in charge, and Meredith Reiss, collections manager, were extremely helpful. Michael Mattis and Judith Hochberg, assisted by Hava Gurevitch at art2art, saved the day with some key last-minute loans to round out the selection. Finally, Mike Allen and Dennis Santella at Affirmation Arts were invaluable in coordinating loans (and much more) on behalf of William Talbott Hillman.

Katie Reilly and her team in publications, particularly Laurel Mitchell and Matthew Newton, were crucial to the production of the catalogue. Our ever-efficient editor Michelle Piranio turned around texts in record time and with helpful corrections; and we owe the design of this

beautiful book to Beverly Joel. Curatorial assistant Hannah Turpin researched a thorough bibliography and facilitated nearly every other aspect of the project. Her unwavering dedication deserves
special recognition.

For the exhibition, Gabriela DiDonna in the registrar's office was a steadying presence as
she oversaw the often-tricky task of moving artworks between institutions. Elizabeth Tufts-Brown
kept diligent track of things once on-site at the museum. Ellen Baxter, chief conservator, helped
ensure that the highest levels of care were provided for these delicate objects. The entire art
preparation and installation team, led by Mark Blatnik, facilitated a smooth and timely installation.
They were guided by a thoughtful exhibition design from Emily Rice, and initially coordinated by
Hannah Silbert.

Projects such as this require a great deal of thinking about our public, and numerous
individuals played key roles in this respect. Michelle Horton and her staff in development conceived
of the best ways to seek support for the exhibition. The marketing team, under the leadership of
Brad Stephenson, developed a captivating branding and advertising strategy to ensure that our
local audiences and those farther afield would know about the show. Perhaps the most meaning-
ful interactions with visitors happen through our education department, where Marilyn Russell
and her colleagues formulated fantastic public programs, tours, and events.

I benefited greatly from the input, advice, and guidance of too many smart individuals to
possibly list here, but several deserve to be called out. Gail Buckland, Kate Bush, Mat Collishaw,
Kate Davies, Graham Hogg, Brian Liddy, Russell Lord, Shasti Lowton, Anne Lyden, Lisa Oppenheim,
Lewis Pollard, Russell Roberts, and Roger Watson all share a piece of the credit for this endeavor.
Finally, as always, I am grateful for the support of my family. Jenn is my ultimate editor, both in
writing and in life, helping me identify what really matters. Sammy keeps me on my toes and
reminds me to appreciate each new discovery.

Dan Leers
Curator of Photography

Published on the occasion of the exhibition *William Henry Fox Talbot and the Promise of Photography* at Carnegie Museum of Art, Pittsburgh, November 18, 2017– February 11, 2018.

Support for the exhibition is generously provided by the William Talbott Hillman Foundation.

Published by
Carnegie Museum of Art
4400 Forbes Avenue
Pittsburgh, Pennsylvania, 15213
www.cmoa.org

CARNEGIE MUSEUM OF ART

ONE OF THE FOUR CARNEGIE MUSEUMS
OF PITTSBURGH

Editors: Michelle Piranio, Katie Reilly
Design: Beverly Joel, pulp, ink.
Printer: die Keure, Bruges, Belgium

ISBN 978-0-8803-9060-6

Library of Congress Cataloging-in-Publication Data
    Names: Leers, Dan, author. | Schaaf, Larry J. (Larry John), 1947– | Carnegie
        Museum of Art, organizer, host institution.
    Title: William Henry Fox Talbot and the promise of photography / Dan Leers;
        with contributions by Larry J. Schaaf.
    Description: Pittsburgh, Pennsylvania : Carnegie Museum of Art, 2017. |
        "Published on the occasion of the exhibition William Henry Fox Talbot
        and the Promise of Photography at Carnegie Museum of Art,
        Pittsburgh, November 18, 2017–February 11, 2018." | Includes
        bibliographical references.
    Identifiers: LCCN 2017035902 | ISBN 9780880390606 (alk. paper)
    Subjects: LCSH: Talbot, William Henry Fox, 1800–1877—Exhibitions.
    Classification: LCC TR647 .T35 2017 | DDC 770.74/74886—dc23 LC record
    available at https://lccn.loc.gov/2017035902

Front cover: *Buckler Fern*, ca. 1839 (detail). Photogenic drawing negative, 8⅝ × 7 in. (22 × 17.9 cm) (irregular). Carnegie Museum of Art, Pittsburgh, Gift of William Talbott Hillman

Back cover: *Bust of Venus on a Round Tabletop*, early 1840s. Salted paper print from a calotype negative, 3⅞ × 3 in. (9.9 × 7.5 cm). Carnegie Museum of Art, Pittsburgh, Gift of William Talbott Hillman, 2017.30.1

Endpapers: *Articles of China*, 1844 (detail). Salted paper print from a calotype negative, 5½ × 7³⁄₁₆ in. (14 × 18.2 cm) image; 7⅜ × 8¾ in. (18.7 × 22.2 cm) sheet. Carnegie Museum of Art, Pittsburgh, Purchased with funds provided by the William Talbott Hillman Foundation, 2017.2.2

Frontispiece: *Nicolaas Henneman Showing an Album to Charles Porter*, ca. 1845. Salted paper print from a calotype negative, 5¹⁵⁄₁₆ × 7⅝ in. (15.1 × 19.3 cm) image; 6 × 7¹¹⁄₁₆ in. (15.3 × 19.6 cm) sheet. The Metropolitan Museum of Art, New York, Bequest of Maurice B. Sendak, 2012, 2013.159.63

Illustration Credits
Many of the images are protected by copyright and may not be available for further reproduction without permission of the artist or copyright holder. Every reasonable attempt has been made to identify owners of copyright. Errors or omissions will be corrected in subsequent editions.

Front and back covers: Carnegie Museum of Art, Photo: Bryan Conley

Frontispiece: The Metropolitan Museum of Art, New York

p. 8: Carnegie Museum of Art, Photo: Bryan Conley

Leers essay:
Fig. 1: © The British Library Board. Talbot Photo 4; Fig. 2: National Science & Media Museum/Science & Society Picture Library; Fig. 3: © The British Library Board. Talbot Photo 10 (12); Fig. 4: Courtesy of George Eastman Museum; Fig. 5: © Museum of the History of Science, University of Oxford; Fig. 6: National Science & Media Museum/Science & Society Picture Library; Fig. 7: Carnegie Museum of Art, Photo: Bryan Conley; Fig. 8: Digital image courtesy of the Getty's Open Content Program; Fig. 9: The J. Paul Getty Museum, Los Angeles

pp. 20–21: The Metropolitan Museum of Art, New York

Plates:
pp. 22, 29, 58, 71, 83: The Metropolitan Museum of Art, New York; pp. 25, 33, 61, 75, 77, 81: Carnegie Museum of Art, Photo: Bryan Conley; pp. 27, 31, 37, 45, 48, 49, 51, 52, 63, 67, 72, 79, 85: Hans P. Kraus Jr., New York; pp. 34, 39, 41, 46, 53, 57: Private collection, courtesy of Hans P. Kraus Jr., New York; pp. 43, 65: Collection of Michael Mattis and Judith Hochberg, New York; pp. 55, 69: Courtesy of Phillips

p. 89: Digital image courtesy of the Getty's Open Content Program

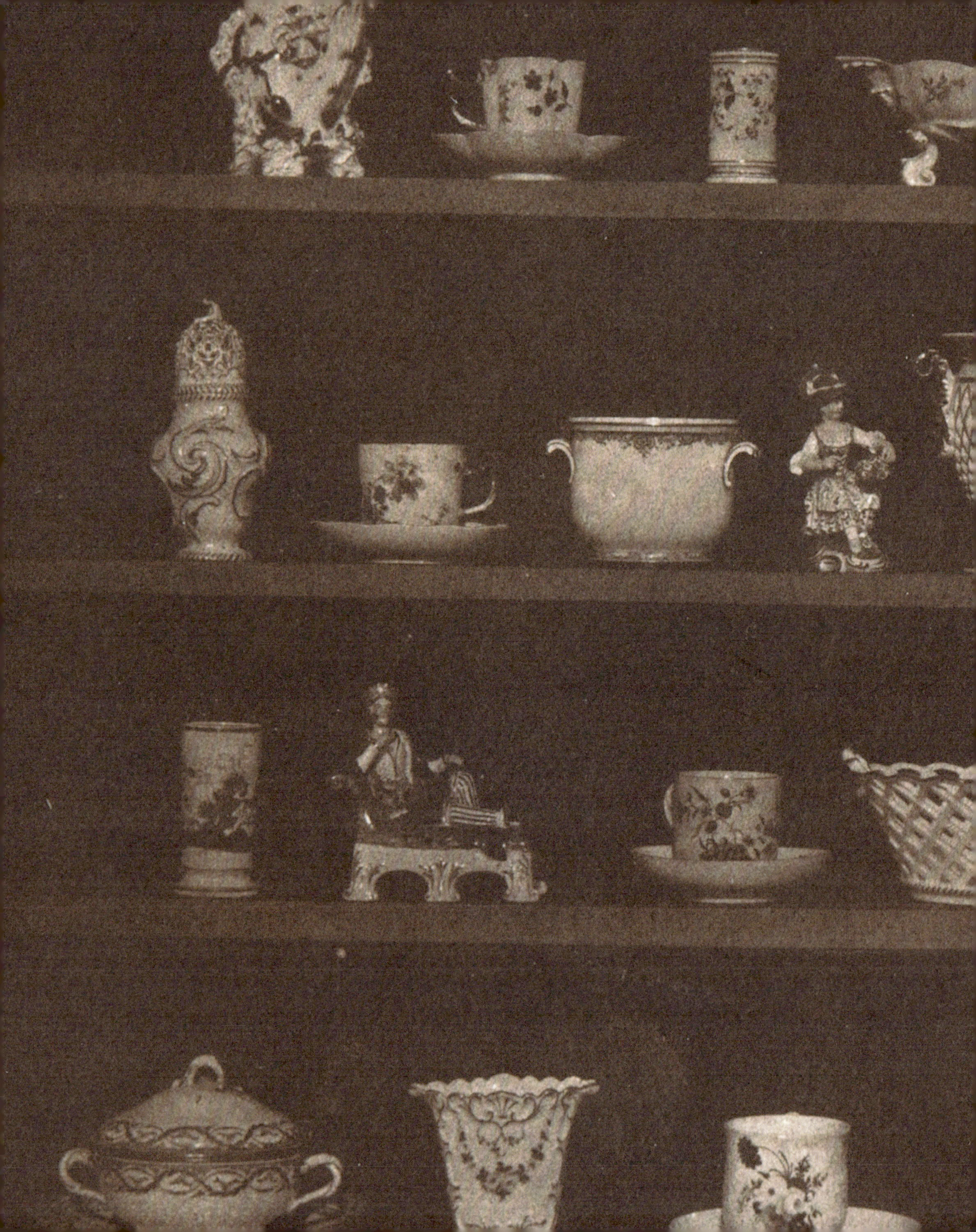